Oxford Bookworms

Teacher's Guide

OXFORD UNIVERSITY PRESS

Oxford Bookworms
Series Editors: Tricia Hedge and Jennifer Bassett

Oxford University Press
Walton Street
Oxford OX2 6DP

Oxford New York Athens Auckland Bangkok
Bombay Calcutta Cape Town Dar es Salaam Delhi
Florence Hong Kong Istanbul Karachi
Kuala Lumpur Madras Madrid Melbourne
Mexico City Nairobi Paris Singapore
Taipai Tokyo Toronto

and associated companies in
Berlin Ibadan

Oxford and *Oxford English*
are trade marks of Oxford University Press

ISBN 0 19 422899 1

Illustrations from *The Elephant Man* by Nick Harris, from *Sherlock
Holmes – Short Stories* by Alan Morrison, and from *Tales of Mystery
and Imagination* by Ian Miller. All other illustrations supplied by
Creative Intelligence, Bristol.
Board Game designed by Creative Intelligence, Bristol.

The *Answers to the exercises* were compiled by Christine Lindop,
Running a class library and *Using cassettes* were written by Elizabeth
White, and the activities were supplied by Tim Vicary, Margaret Naudi,
Clare West, Diane Mowat, and Jennifer Bassett.

Printed in England by St Edmundsbury Press, Bury St Edmunds, Suffolk

CONTENTS

INTRODUCTION

This booklet is designed to make it easier for you to use the Oxford Bookworms series of graded readers with your students. It contains answers to the exercises in all Bookworms published before June 1994. Updates will become available at regular intervals as new titles are published. The answer key is arranged in two parts: the Black Series followed by the Green Series. Within each section, the answers are grouped by stage, in alphabetical order of title. There is also a complete alphabetical index by title at the end of the booklet.

We know that teachers have many different ways of exploiting graded readers. Some of you may adopt a single title and use it as your class reader for the term; others may prefer to have a class library where students can borrow a variety of different books. This second option is rather more complex to administer, so we have included in this Teacher's Guide some advice from an experienced teacher on running a class library. We hope you will find it useful. More background information can be found in *Using Readers in Language Teaching* by Tricia Hedge in the *Essential Language Teaching Series*, published by Macmillan.

Many Bookworms are now also available on cassette, and after the article on class libraries, you will find a short section on getting the most out of these recordings.

Finally, it is increasingly recognized that readers are a valuable language resource that can be exploited in many different ways, in addition to straightforward reading comprehension. We therefore asked some of our authors, who are also experienced teachers, to provide examples of activities that they have done with their students. You will find these after the answer key. We have included activities for a title at each stage of Bookworms, so whatever the level of your students, we hope you will find some ideas that you can use. If this inspires you to create activities of your own, many more ideas for exploiting graded readers may be found in *Class Readers* by Jean Greenwood in the *Resource Books for Teachers* series published by Oxford University Press.

Good luck and good reading!

RUNNING A CLASS LIBRARY

ORDERING YOUR LIBRARY

To start with, a class library has to have a good selection of good books. You need enough books to make sure that everyone will find something they want to read, and you need a good variety of titles and genres. Remember that your idea of what is a good book might not be the same as the students'; if you can, get your students to help choose the books from publishers' catalogues. You also need enough books at the right levels for your students to read with fluency.

Some schools pay for their class library by getting students to buy in to the library; each new student chooses and pays for one book, which then becomes part of the library. This helps students to feel that they are taking part in running the library, and that it is their resource.

If possible, buy the cassettes with the books; students always like using them, and they might encourage even reluctant readers to make use of the library.

PREPARING BOOKS FOR THE LIBRARY

Once you have the books, arrange them into levels; this helps students to choose books at the right level of difficulty, and allows them a sense of progress as they move up through the levels. The Oxford Bookworm stages are identified by the coloured 'worm' on the cover. If you have books from several different series, you may like to construct your own grading system using coloured labels. The chart in the back of the Oxford Graded Readers catalogue will give you information about how the levels of the different Oxford series relate to each other, in terms not only of vocabulary and structure, but also number of pages.

If you put plastic jackets on the books, they will last almost twice as long.

DISPLAYING BOOKS

Even if your school has a general library, it is best to keep a set of graded readers as a class library in the English classroom. Students ought to see the library as an important part of their learning, and you need to make it very easy for students to choose and borrow books. Don't lock the books away in a cupboard; keep them in a prominent part of the class and make sure that the books are visible and available. If students can't see the books, they aren't going to clamour to read them.

Graded readers tend to be thin books with little room for detail on the spine of the book, but with covers designed to attract and interest students. Make room to display some or all of the books with the covers on show. Since the books are not very heavy, you don't need a full-size bookcase for this; you can display the books on wire racks, or even on thin strips of wood attached to the wall of the classroom.

TRAINING STUDENTS TO USE THE LIBRARY

Even with the books brightly on display in the classroom, you need to present the idea of the library to students and to explain how they can use the library to get the most out of the books. Take one lesson to explain your library system, to talk about the books and to explain how reading from the library will help your students to improve their reading skills in English and their language ability.

Most of all, you need to make sure that students don't try to read books which are too difficult for them to read fluently. Your students should be reading for pleasure – and if they are looking up every third word,

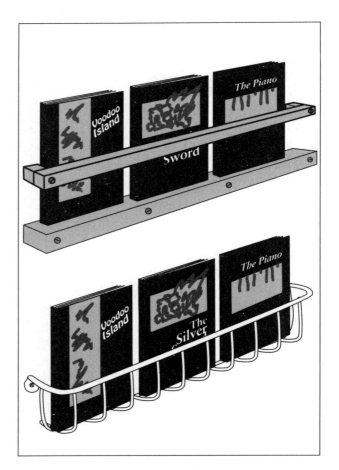

Display racks

BORROWERS' CHART A = INTERESTING B = EXCITING C = HAPPY D = SAD
E = EASY F = DIFFICULT G = DIDN'T LIKE IT

TITLES	THE ELEPHANT MAN	OLIVER TWIST	THE COLDEST PLACE ON EARTH
NAME	Marcia	Rosario	Kaori
DATE BORROWED	18/3/94	12/3/94	15/3/94
DATE BACK	23/3/94	14/3/94	17/3/94
OPINION	E A D	F A	A B D F
NAME	Philippe	Kaori	
DATE BORROWED	3/4/94	23/3/94	
DATE BACK	14/4/94		
OPINION	E C		

there is little pleasure involved, and it will take them a long time to get through a book. Emphasize this, because students often try to read at the outer level of their ability, even when they are reading a novel. You can recommend a level for students to try, or you can get them to 'taste' the books for themselves by opening them in the middle, reading two pages, and then stopping to think: *Can I follow the general meaning quite easily? Can I understand about 95% of the words? Am I interested?* And if they can answer yes, the book ought to be about right for them.

It's a good idea to give students some training at an early stage in book-attack skills, so that they will learn to use the help given by the introduction, the blurb, the illustrations and the glossaries.

KEEPING RECORDS

Depending on your school circumstances, you may be able to keep the class library on open access; some books may disappear, but students will be able to borrow books when they like. Otherwise you may have to use class time for students to borrow books from the library. You could appoint one or two students to act as librarians, and even offer them the library fines as payment for the work.

You need to decide what kind of records you are going to keep. The simplest thing is a large wall-chart which you can keep next to the class library. When students borrow a book, they write their name and date borrowed; when they return it, they write the date and an opinion of the book. This can simply be a number or a letter:

A = INTERESTING   B = EXCITING
C = HAPPY   D = SAD   E = EASY
F = DIFFICULT   G = DIDN'T LIKE IT

– or you could leave room for more comment. The chart might look like the one above.

You can also get students to keep a record of their own reading; this can be anything from just a record of the title to a critical report of the book. It will depend on the students' preferred ways of working, and on their level. In general, though, the book record should be quick and easy to complete.

WORKING WITH THE LIBRARY IN CLASS

If you can give some of your class time to working with the class library, students will see the library as more central to their learning; it will also give them a chance to talk about what they are reading, and to compare opinions with their classmates.

Some ideas

Reading Tutorials: if you have time to organize short meetings between teacher and one or two students at a time, this is a good way for you to keep track of what students are reading and what they think of the books, to show your interest in their reading, and to help them with their reading.

Reading Syndicates: this is a way of encouraging students to talk about what they are reading. You need several small sets of the same book. Divide the class into groups of five, and give each group the same set of five different books so that each member of the group is reading something different. So, for example, student A in each group is reading *The Piano*, while student B is reading *Jane Eyre*. Give them a week or two to finish the books, then arrange class discussions. First, group all the students A together so that they can compare opinions about *The Piano*, while all the B students talk about their book, and so on with each book. Then re-group the syndicates so that you have ABCD and E together, and they tell each other about what they have been reading, and recommend their books to each other.

DEAR time: this is an idea adapted from L1 reading. The way it works is very simple: everyone in the class always has to have a book with them: at some point in the lesson, you announce fifteen minutes DEAR time, and everybody, including the teacher, Drops Everything And Reads. You do this regularly. Nothing else – but it works. Students begin to get the habit of reading, and to read more outside class too.

Exploiting the library: as the term or the year goes on, more and more students will have read many of the titles in the library, and you can exploit this partially shared knowledge in your classwork. Get students to write library quizzes, to be answered by small groups; play charades with the titles of the books; get students to act out scenes from the books for others to guess; play drama games where all the students act as a character from one of the books they have read, while others guess their identity. You can, of course, also use the open-ended questions in Part C of the exercises at the back of each Bookworm, and you will find some further suggestions for classroom activities at the end of this booklet.

KEEPING IT GOING

A class library needs to be kept alive, and students need encouragement to carry on reading. With luck, a sense of progress and increased fluency in reading will persuade students to read more and more – but you can help to make sure this happens.

Keep renewing the stock of books in your class library, so that students see a different selection of books to choose from. If you monitor what students are reading, you can see what types of books are most popular, and buy more of them. And from time to time you need to weed out the books which haven't been read, or which nobody liked, or which are falling to pieces. Old and uninteresting books which stay on library shelves make the whole library look less attractive to students.

The single most important thing in keeping a library going, and keeping students reading, is the continued interest and enthusiasm of the teacher. Show an interest in what students are reading, talk about the library, discuss the books with students, include references to the books in your classwork – and read the books. Enjoy yourselves.

USING CASSETTES

Everybody likes being read to, and students enjoy listening to the text of their books on cassette. Many of the Bookworms have accompanying cassettes with the whole text of the books; if you can, buy the cassettes with the books and use them together. They are particularly useful at lower levels, where they can help students to recognize words in written and spoken form – but they are always very popular with students at all levels.

In class, you can use the cassettes to help to advertize the library to your students, by playing interesting excerpts from several cassettes and displaying the covers of the books, asking students to guess which excerpt comes from which book. Or you can give out photocopies of the first few pages of a book and ask students to read and follow the text while they listen to the text (this means that everyone is reading at the same slow comfortable speed); stop the cassette at a crucial moment, and then ask students to predict what will happen next. In this way, students will be interested to find out the rest of the story, and more willing to read the book.

Most of all, though, try to lend the cassettes to students with the books. Even reluctant readers will often take to reading if they can listen to the text at the same time, and you will probably find that the books with cassettes are the most popular books in the library. You may want to charge students a small deposit on the cassettes, to make sure that you don't lose them.

Some students may also like to listen to the cassettes without the accompanying book, perhaps on their personal stereo or car stereo, in situations where reading would not be possible. This will help develop students' listening comprehension, and also, most importantly, will encourage them to enjoy stories. You may find that as they listen to more stories, they become more motivated to read, as well.

Many Bookworms are already available on cassette. These are marked with an asterisk in the Index. Cassettes are in preparation for many more of the titles, so please consult your local bookseller for an up-to-date list.

Elizabeth White

ANSWERS TO
THE EXERCISES

Answers are given here to all exercises in Section A, which are comprehension exercises, and to those in Section B, which are exercises based on discourse features such as linking, subordination, ellipsis and reference. Some of these exercises can often be done as pair or group work in class. The answers given here are sometimes only models, as there may be several acceptable answers to some kinds of exercise.

No answers are given to the exercises in Section C, as these are activities designed to stimulate creative oral or written responses from the students.

Answer Key
BLACK SERIES

The Coldest Place on Earth

A Checking your understanding

Chapters 1–3
1 Titus Oates.
2 Captain Scott.
3 Olav Bjaaland.
4 Roald Amundsen.
5 Johansen.
6 Amundsen.
7 Bjaaland.
8 A newspaper man in Wellington, New Zealand.
9 Scott.
10 Oates.

Chapters 4–6
1 T   2 T   3 F   4 F   5 T
6 T   7 F   8 F   9 T

Chapters 7–8
1 Oates.
2 Meares.
3 Wisting.
4 Teddy Evans and his men.
5 Bjaaland and Amundsen.
6 The Norwegians.
7 Oates.
8 Scott.
9 Bowers.

Chapters 9–10
1 Amundsen.
2 Scott.
3 Scott's wife Kathleen.
4 Oates.
5 Oates.
6 Scott.

B Working with language

Exercise 1
1 & e   2 & c   3 & g   4 & f   5 & a
6 & d   7 & b

Exercise 2
1 Scott didn't make enough depots, so his men were hungry.
2 The men's feet hurt, because their boots were bad.

3 The ponies started at ten o'clock and then the dogs started at eleven.
4 The dogs started later but they ran faster.
5 Seven ponies died when they fell through the ice into the sea.

The Elephant Man

A Checking your understanding

Chapter 1
1 At the London Hospital.
2 A horrible, ugly picture of a man.
3 The Elephant Man.
4 Because he could not walk well.

Chapter 2
1 Because it was early in the morning.
2 Because he wore an enormous hat, with a cloth in front of his face, and a long coat.
3 In a cab.
4 He looked at his head, arms, legs, and body very carefully.

Chapters 3–4
1 Because he had Dr Treves's card in his hand.
2 Because Silcock took his £50.
3 His mother.
4 She screamed, dropped his food on the floor, and ran out of the room.
5 Because nobody could look at him there.

Chapters 5–6
1 F   2 F   3 T   4 F   5 T

Chapter 7
1 In bed.
2 No.
3 Yes.
4 He gave it to the hospital.

B Working with language

Exercise 1
1 . . . he had Dr Treves's card in his hand.
2 . . . Silcock took it.
3 . . . many people were afraid of him.
4 . . . we need some money.
5 . . . reading, and talking about books.

Exercise 2
1 & 11   2 & 9   3 & 7   4 & 12   5 & 10   6 & 8

Love or Money?

A Checking your understanding

Chapter 1
1 Jackie.
2 Molly.
3 Diane.
4 Jackie.
5 Peter Hobbs.

Chapter 2
1 Albert.
2 Diane.
3 Roger.
4 Molly.
5 Diane.

Chapter 3
1 Diane.
2 Diane.
3 On Thursday.
4 No.

Chapter 4
1 T   2 F   3 F   4 T

Chapter 5
1 Roger.
2 The empty bottle of sleeping tablets.
3 The gardener.
4 Uncle Albert, Jackie, Diane, Roger, Peter Hobbs, and Tom Briggs.

Chapter 6
1 Peter Hobbs.
2 Inspector Walsh.
3 Tom Briggs.
4 Tom Briggs.

Chapter 7
1 Diane.
2 In Diane's bag.
3 In Tom Briggs' house.
4 Jackie.

B Working with language

Exercise 1
1 Jackie felt angry because her sister always asked for money.
2 Roger got out of bed, and then he opened the door quietly.
3 Inspector Walsh always felt cold so he wore a coat.
4 Diane opened the back door and then she went out with the dogs.
5 I'm losing money on this farm so I need more land.
6 I don't need your help because Mother always helps me.

Exercise 2
3, 1, 5, 6, 2, 4

Mary Queen of Scots

A Checking your understanding

Chapters 1–2
1 T   2 T   3 F   4 F   5 T
6 F   7 T   8 F   9 F   10 T

Chapters 3–4
1 Queen Elizabeth.
2 Mary.
3 Henry Darnley.
4 The Earl of Moray's friends.
5 Darnley.
6 Lord Ruthven.
7 David Riccio.
8 Darnley.
9 Mary.
10 Mary.

Chapters 5–7
1 Darnley.
2 Mary.
3 Mary, Darnley, and Bess Curle.
4 Lord Bothwell.
5 Darnley.
6 Darnley.
7 One of Lord Bothwell's men.
8 People in Edinburgh.
9 Lord Kirkcaldy.
10 Lord Bothwell.

Chapters 8–9
1 T   2 F   3 T   4 F   5 F
6 T   7 T   8 F

B Working with language

Exercise 1
Mary came back to Scotland when her husband died.
The Scots lords hated Riccio so they killed him.
Mary asked Darnley to help but he didn't like the work.
Mary went away with Bothwell because he had an army.
Darnley's body was in the garden after Kirk o'Field blew up.
Mary went to England to ask Elizabeth for an army.
Elizabeth kept Mary in prison because she couldn't make up her mind.

Exercise 2
1 John Knox didn't like Mary because she was a Catholic and a woman.
2 Mary liked Darnley so she married him.
3 Bothwell met Mary outside Edinburgh and took her to his castle.
4 Mary liked Riccio but Moray and Darnley didn't like him.
5 Darnley was afraid when Mary wasn't with him.

The Monkey's Paw

A Checking your understanding

Chapter 1
1 Mr and Mrs White and their son Herbert.
2 Mr and Mrs White were old. They had a young son called Herbert. They didn't have very much money, but they were a happy family.

Chapter 2
1 For twenty-one years.
2 Because it brought unhappiness to people.
3 Because it could give three wishes to three people.
4 He wished for a fast car, but his wife and son died in an accident in it.

Chapters 3–4
1 T   2 T   3 F   4 F   5 F

Chapter 5
1 He was a tall well-dressed man who worked for Maw and Meggins.
2 Because Herbert was in the machinery for a long time.
3 He was afraid.

Chapter 6
1 They were rich, but they felt unhappy.
2 She wanted to wish for Herbert to come back.
3 He didn't want to see Herbert's body after the accident.

Chapter 7
1 F   2 T   3 F   4 F

B Working with language

Exercise 1
1 . . . they were exciting and interesting.
2 . . . felt afraid because the monkey's paw moved.
3 . . . he thought it was a strange and wonderful place.
4 . . . he saw a face at the window.
5 . . . he didn't want to see Herbert.
6 . . . she wanted to see her son.
7 . . . Mr White wished for him to go away.

Exercise 2
1 & 11   2 & 7   3 & 12   4 & 8   5 & 9   6 & 10

Mutiny on the Bounty

A Checking your understanding

Chapters 1–2
1 Peter Heywood.
2 John Adams.
3 William Bligh.
4 Otoo, the king of Tahiti.
5 William Bligh.
6 Fletcher Christian.
7 John Adams.
8 William Bligh.
9 John Adams.
10 Peter Heywood.

Chapter 3
1 It was seven metres long.
2 Nineteen.
3 About seven thousand kilometres.
4 Forty-one days.
5 Bread, breadfruit, meat, coconuts, birds, rum, and water.

Chapters 4–5
1 F   2 T   3 F   4 F   5 T   6 F

B Working with language

Exercise 1
1 Captain Bligh was a good sailor but some of his officers didn't like him.
2 The king did not let Peter Heywood die because he was only a boy in the mutiny.
3 Captain Bligh was very angry when the sailors put him in the launch.
4 Thursday Christian talked to Captain Pipon and Captain Staines and he took them to see John Adams.

Exercise 2
1 & 6   2 & 5   3 & 7   4 & 8

One-Way Ticket

A Checking your understanding

The Girl with Green Eyes
1 Julie.
2 The woman with the children.
3 Julie.
4 Bill.
5 The tall dark man.

The Girl with Green Eyes
1 The man in the brown hat.
2 Because they were boring.
3 A book about famous towns in Italy.
4 The little girl and her mother.
5 Because he knew a woman once with green eyes, and she gave him a bad time.

South for the Winter
1 F   2 T   3 F   4 T

South for the Winter
1 Because she wasn't hungry and she wanted to sleep.
2 At the Hotel Marmara on Saturday night at eight o'clock.
3 200,000 US dollars.
4 Carol.
5 They wanted to go to Australia.

Mr Harris and the Night Train

1 They were always noisy.
2 Because he had no money.
3 He took them from Elena's room.
4 He laughed and laughed.
5 There was nobody there.
6 About eighty years ago.
7 She jumped off the train.
8 By bus.

B Working with language

South for the Winter

4, 7, 1, 8, 6, 3, 5, 2

Mr Harris and the Night Train

1 & 6   2 & 8   3 & 5   4 & 7

The Phantom of the Opera

A Checking your understanding

Chapters 1–2

1 More than 2,500.
2 Box 5.
3 Some stage workers.
4 20,000 francs a month.
5 La Carlotta.

Chapters 3–4

1 They loved her, and thought she was wonderful, the best singer in the world.
2 Four years ago, when he was on holiday in Brittany.
3 Because he wanted to see her lover.
4 They were fools.
5 He wanted to watch the opera from Box 5.

Chapters 5–6

1 F   2 T   3 T   4 F   5 F

Chapters 7–8

1 Christine.
2 The Phantom of the Opera.
3 The Persian.
4 Comte Philippe de Chagny.
5 Meg Giry.

Chapters 9–10

1 They went through a hole in the wall behind the mirror.
2 Because they were in Erik's torture room and they couldn't get out of the room alive.
3 Because Christine kissed Erik lovingly on his ugly mouth.
4 Because the Phantom was dead.
5 *Open answer.*

B Working with language

Exercise 1

1 & 8   2 & 5   3 & 7   4 & 6

Exercise 2

3, 5, 8, 4, 7, 1, 6, 2

The President's Murderer

A Checking your understanding

The First Day

1 Five or six.
2 About two kilometres.
3 Three months ago.
4 Twenty-four hours ago.

The Second Day

1 T   2 F   3 F   4 T

The Third Day

1 Her friend George.
2 The woman from the post office.
3 Marta.
4 Adam.

The Fourth Day

1 To buy some food.
2 The lorry driver.
3 He wrote a book about the old President.
4 Nothing.

The Fifth Day

1 F   2 T   3 F   4 T

The Sixth Day

1 He wanted her to wait for a year, then leave the country secretly with the children.
2 Because Alex Dinon was dead.
3 The new President needed a murderer quickly, so the police found a murderer for him.
4 Because he didn't stop asking questions.

B Working with language

Exercise 1

1 . . . they could find him in the dark.
2 . . . he couldn't find Alex Dinon.
3 . . . he saw an old woman in front of him.
4 . . . she didn't like the police.
5 . . . the police arrived.
6 . . . she told him nothing.

Exercise 2

5, 2, 9, 6, 8, 3, 1, 4, 7

Under the Moon

A Checking your understanding

Chapter 1

1 Kiah.
2 Rilla.
3 Captain Seru.
4 Captain Seru.
5 Kiah.

Chapter 2

1 Rilla.
2 A guard.
3 Kiah.
4 Commander Zadak.
5 Commander Zadak.

Chapter 3

1 Mars.
2 A guard.
3 A cat.
4 A television, three computers and five telephones.
5 Bel.

Chapter 4

1 F   2 T   3 F   4 T   5 F

Chapter 5

1 Gog.
2 Gog.
3 Rilla.
4 Captain Seru.
5 Seru's brother.

Chapter 6

1 T   2 T   3 F   4 F   5 T

B Working with language

Exercise 1

1 The guard opened the gate and then Zadak went in.
2 A lot of prisoners slept on the floor because there were no beds or chairs.
3 'I talk to Gog about the AOL but he never listens.'
4 'All these people are in prison because Gog doesn't like them.'
5 Zadak smiled but his blue eyes were cold.
6 The cat jumped at Zadak and then Zadak hit the cat.

Exercise 2

3, 5, 2, 4, 6, 1

White Death

A Checking your understanding

Chapter 1

1 Anna Harland.
2 The man at the prison.
3 Sarah.
4 The man at the prison.

Chapter 2

1 T   2 F   3 F   4 F

Chapter 3

1 The police lawyer.
2 Anna.
3 The judge.
4 Mr Cheng.

Chapter 4

1 T   2 T   3 T   4 F

Chapter 5

1 Stephen.
2 Hassan.
3 Mr Cheng.
4 Stephen.

Chapter 6

1 F   2 T   3 F

Chapter 8

1 Sarah.
2 Inspector Aziz.
3 Anna.
4 Inspector Aziz.

B Working with language

Exercise 1

1 . . . she's going to court tomorrow.'
2 . . . he has two daughters.'
3 . . . she worked for six months in a hospital.
4 . . . people bring heroin into the country.
5 . . . the plane arrived.

Exercise 2

Anna Harland stood outside the hotel.
Anna walked into the hotel and went upstairs.
Anna knocked on the door of a bedroom.
Anna said: 'I need your help. Please get up.'
Anna opened her handbag and showed Stephen a tube of toothpaste.
Stephen looked at the tube of toothpaste and stood up.
Stephen opened the door quickly and then stopped.
Inspector Aziz stood at the door.
Inspector Aziz put a hand on Stephen's arm.

The Witches of Pendle

A Checking your understanding

Chapter 1

1 Jennet Device.
2 James Device.
3 Alizon Device.
4 John Law.
5 The villagers.

Chapter 2

1 At Read Hall, seven miles from Newchurch.
2 Nearly eighty years old.
3 Twenty years ago.
4 To the prison at Lancaster Castle.
5 A sheep.

Chapter 3

1 T   2 F   3 T   4 F

Chapter 4

1 Jennet's mother.

2 Judge Bromley.
3 James Device.
4 Mr Nowell's servant.
5 Mr Webster.

B Working with language

Exercise 1

1 . . . sleep on the cold floor.
2 . . . it sat quietly all year and watched her.
3 . . . it was always hungry.
4 . . . he's very ill.'
5 . . . she was a witch.

Exercise 2

1 & 3   5 & 2   4 & 6

Exercise 3

1 We went along the river and then it began to rain.
2 Mr Nowell looked up from his book when we finished eating.
3 James liked Mr Nowell because Mr Nowell didn't shout at him.
4 'You're my daughter but you're not the daughter of my husband.'

Exercise 4

6 & 1   4 & 2   3 & 5

STAGE TWO

Dead Man's Island

A Checking your understanding

Chapter 1

1 His plane crashed in the sea.
2 Seventeen.
3 Because she felt unhappy and angry.
4 She began to take drugs.
5 Because she wanted to begin a new life, and be a new person.
6 At the Savoy Hotel.

Chapter 2

1 Carol.
2 Tony.
3 Greta.
4 Mr Ross.
5 Carol's mother.

Chapter 3

1 F   2 T   3 F   4 T   5 F

Chapter 4

1 Carol.
2 Mr Ross.
3 Tony Duncan and Mrs Ross.

Chapter 5

1 James Duncan.

2 Mr Ross's father and mother.
3 Fifteen.
4 He put his guitar and some clothes in his car, then he pushed the car over a cliff and burned it.
5 At the end of the summer.

B Working with language

Exercise 1

1 . . . her father died.
2 . . . had to leave the college.
3 . . . she telephoned Greta Ross.
4 . . . his last secretary was in hospital.
5 . . . was coming out of a door.
6 . . . Mr Ross didn't like people to take pictures of him.
7 . . . hid the key in the plant pot next to the door.
8 . . . didn't answer, but ran into her room and closed the door.

Exercise 2

3, 5, 1, 10, 6, 9, 2, 4, 8, 7

The Death of Karen Silkwood

A Checking your understanding

Chapters 1–3

1 Twenty-eight.
2 Because she was bringing them some important papers and photographs.
3 She had to put uranium into fuel rods.
4 In the coffee bar at the factory.

Chapters 4–6

1 F   2 F   3 T   4 T   5 F   6 T

Chapters 7–8

1 The Union leaders.
2 The other workers.
3 Drew.
4 Paula.
5 The men in white.

Chapters 9–11

1 He took her to his home.
2 Someone put something radioactive into her bag before she left the factory.
3 He thought it was a very dangerous thing to do.
4 The Union.
5 To get the brown envelope with the papers and photographs.
6 Drew, Pete, and the journalist from the New York Times.

B Working with language

Exercise 1

1 . . . the pay was much better than a secretary's pay and the work was more interesting.
2 . . . the alarm made a terrible noise.

3 . . . they knew she wanted to change things at the factory.
4 . . . they wrote to the Union leaders in Washington.
5 . . . the government will close your factory.'

Exercise 2
6, 3, 5, 10, 9, 1, 2, 8, 7, 4

Ear-rings from Frankfurt

A Checking your understanding

Chapter 1
1 F   2 T   3 F   4 T   5 T   6 T

Chapter 2
1 Dr Gibson.
2 Jennifer.
3 Detective Barrett.
4 Wendy.

Chapter 3
1 He bought and sold cars, furniture, old pictures, and jewellery.
2 He wanted her to get three small boxes from his friends and bring them back to England.
3 She thought it was stolen jewellery.
4 He went to buy a newspaper, and he also phoned the police.
5 They followed the white Mercedes.
6 He said they were a birthday present.
7 A letter about the 'eggs' (the stolen jewellery).
8 16th April.

Chapter 4
1 The police.
2 Detective Barrett and Detective Edwards.
3 Detective Edwards.
4 Richard.
5 Kelly and two other men.
6 Richard.

B Working with language

Exercise 1
A1 & B6   A2 & B8   A3 & B4   A4 & B2
A5 & B7   A6 & B5   A7 & B3   A8 & B1

Exercise 2
1 Kelly fell and hurt himself, so Jennifer and Claire took him to hospital.
2 Richard could not buy Wendy a present because he had no money.
3 Wendy telephoned Jennifer before she went to her flat.
4 When Barrett went to Jennifer's flat, he asked her a lot of questions.
5 Wendy told the police everything, but they did not believe her.

Grace Darling

A Checking your understanding

Chapter 1
1 T   2 F   3 T

Chapter 2
1 About thirty kilometres south-east of St Abbs Head.
2 William was about fifty, Thomasin was sixty-five, and Grace was about twenty-two.
3 They lit the big oil lantern.
4 In Bamburgh, on the mainland.

Chapters 3–4
1 They were too old, and one of them was broken.
2 A little light flashing.
3 Because he needed her to help him.
4 Because the sounds of the wind and the sea were too loud.
5 Twenty metres high.

Chapters 5–6
1 T   2 F   3 F   4 T   5 F   6 T

Chapters 7–9
1 Thomas Buchanan.
2 Daniel Donovan.
3 William Darling.
4 Thomasin Darling.
5 Grace.
6 Mrs Dawson.
7 Daniel Donovan.

Chapter 10
1 More than a kilometre.
2 Five (with Grace and her father).
3 They died of cold.
4 Daniel Donovan and Thomas Buchanan.

B Working with language

Exercise 1
1 . . . it was a good modern ship.
2 . . . one of the engines stopped.
3 . . . will all drown!'
4 . . . there was always work on a lighthouse.
5 . . . was nearly asleep.
6 . . . only took five the first time.

Exercise 2
1 & 12   2 & 10   3 & 14   4 & 8
5 & 13   6 & 9   7 & 11

The Love of a King

A Checking your understanding

Chapters 1–2
1 T   2 F   3 T   4 F   5 F

Chapters 3–4

1 He went away to fight.
2 He was friendly and interested in people.
3 Because she thought he would talk about something more interesting than central heating.
4 Because they were afraid of him.

Chapters 5–6

1 In Baltimore, USA.
2 Her first husband, Winfield Spencer.
3 Three.
4 She didn't know what would happen to her.

Chapters 7–8

1 Wallis.
2 Ernest Simpson.
3 Gordon Lang, the Archbishop of Canterbury.
4 Edward.
5 Stanley Baldwin, the Prime Minister.
6 Queen Mary.

Chapters 9–10

1 Winston Churchill.
2 Edward.
3 George VI.
4 Wallis.

Chapters 11–12

1 In Paris.
2 Wallis.
3 For fourteen years.
4 To be happy deep inside your heart.

B Working with language

Exercise 1

1 . . . came to a small room in Geneva, Switzerland.
2 . . . Wallis and Edward were special to her.
3 . . . he was always lonely and sad.
4 . . . to fight in the First World War.
5 . . . the King took off his shirt to get brown in the sun.
6 . . . he had never seen a King so badly dressed.
7 . . . she kissed her and touched her arm.
8 . . . lived alone in Paris and did not go out.

Exercise 2

Wallis was born in Baltimore.
She married Winfield Spencer when she was twenty.
One night Winfield hit her and locked her in the bathroom.
So she divorced him.
And then she married Ernest Simpson.
In 1933 Wallis and her aunt went skiing in Austria with Edward.
A few months later Edward asked Wallis to marry him.

New Yorkers

A Checking your understanding

The Christmas Presents

1 She bought the cheapest food.
2 Jim's gold watch and Della's hair.
3 To Madame Eloise's shop.
4 To sell her hair.
5 Because he sold the watch to buy Della's combs.

Soapy's Choice

1 F   2 F   3 T   4 T   5 F

A Walk in Amnesia

1 Doctor Volney.
2 Mr Bolder.
3 Edward Pinkhammer.
4 A woman with a sweet voice and beautiful eyes.
5 Elwyn's wife.

Tildy's Moment

1 All the men who came to the restaurant.
2 Tildy.
3 Mr Seeders.
4 Bogle.
5 Aileen.

The Memento

1 Lynnette D'Armande.
2 On a swing in the theatre.
3 Because she was tired of the life and the men.
4 To a little village by the sea on Long Island.
5 One of Miss Ray's yellow garters.

B Working with language

Soapy's Choice

6 & 1   2 & 4   3 & 8   7 & 5

The Memento

1 All the men got very excited because her garter flew off.
2 These men buy you a drink, and then they think they can do what they want!
3 I was tired of the life, so I decided to leave the theatre.
4 Arthur loved a young woman but he never met her.

The Piano

A Checking your understanding

Chapter 1

1 Because she was a newspaper reporter.
2 Because she was a little afraid.
3 In his dressing-room.
4 His wife Linda.

Chapter 2

1 *Open answer.*
2 *Open answer.*

Chapter 3

1 Tony's mother, Mrs Evans.
2 John.

Chapter 4

1 Mr Wood.
2 Linda Wood.
3 Tony.
4 Pip.

Chapter 5

1 F   2 T   3 F   4 F

Chapter 6

1 He taught lessons to the children at the village school.
2 He gave him piano lessons.
3 Mr Gordon gave him free lessons, but Mr and Mrs Wood offered to pay for the College of Music later on.

Chapter 7

1 He had a piano lesson with Mr Gordon and then he practised for two hours.
2 A new suit, a shirt and a pair of shoes.
3 Because the new shoes were too small.
4 He put his feet in warm water.

B Working with language

Exercise 1

1 One night during the summer holidays Mr Gordon wanted a book.
2 Mr Gordon visited the farm and talked to Mr and Mrs Wood.
3 She was usually a quiet woman, but her eyes were bright and excited.
4 I can find another farm boy but good musicians are special people.

Exercise 2

1 It was an exciting story and he told it well.
2 I worked hard but I enjoyed every minute.
3 He knew that he was the winner because he saw his photograph in the paper the next day.
4 They looked at the rubbish and then they looked at each other.

Sherlock Holmes Short Stories

A Checking your understanding

The Speckled Band

1 Dr Grimesby Roylott.
2 Julia Stoner.
3 Gipsies.
4 Sherlock Holmes and Dr Watson.

The Speckled Band

1 £250 every year.
2 India.
3 Because Julia smelt the smoke from her stepfather's cigarettes when she was in her bedroom.
4 An Indian snake.

A Scandal in Bohemia

1 The King of Bohemia.
2 Sherlock Holmes.
3 Irene Adler.
4 Godfrey Norton.
5 Irene Norton.

A Scandal in Bohemia

1 T   2 F   3 F   4 F   5 T

The Five Orange Pips

1 Elias.
2 When he was twelve.
3 Pondicherry in India, Dundee in Scotland, and East London.
4 Ku Klux Klan.

The Five Orange Pips

1 T   2 T   3 F   4 F

B Working with language

The Speckled Band

We'll take a room in a hotel in the village.
Sherlock Holmes was listening with his eyes closed.
She died two years ago and that's why I'm here.
The police couldn't understand why my sister died.

A Scandal in Bohemia

1 I'm happy to see you, because I've got something to show you.
2 She's a beautiful woman, but she can be as hard as a man.
3 I know that she will send this photograph to the Saxe-Meningen family, and then there will be a terrible scandal.
4 I couldn't miss this, Watson, so I jumped into a third taxi.

Voodoo Island

A Checking your understanding

Chapters 1–2

1 T   2 F   3 T   4 T

Chapter 3

1 Because his business was going well and he was making a lot of money.
2 To build shops, and perhaps a hotel and some more houses.
3 Because the sea was on the south and east sides, and the land on the north side was too wet.
4 Because there was a graveyard there.

Chapters 4–5

1 Because his village was not quiet any more.
2 To the graveyard.
3 Tim Atty, who perhaps was the houngan, and Baron Samedi.
4 Workers from Conway Construction.

Chapters 6–7

1 By bus.
2 Bussy.
3 i) To live in a big house with lots of rooms ii) Lots of people to clean the rooms
  iii) Lots of people to bring him food iv) A lot of money in the bank v) He didn't want to work.
4 His secretary Marie, and his workers Pierre and Henri.

Chapter 8

1 The men from Conway Construction.
2 Kee.
3 Conway.
4 Marie.
5 Kee's grandfather.
6 Conway.

Chapter 9

1 T   2 F   3 F   4 T

B Working with language

Exercise 1

1 & 10   2 & 7   3 & 9   4 & 8   5 & 6

Exercise 2

At first Kee was happy because he thought Conway was a good man.
But one day he went back to the graveyard.
Kee was angry when he saw the men building houses there.
When night came Kee asked the voodoo spirits to help him.
The spirits brought the wind and the rain.
Conway heard the wind and rain outside the window.
Then he went to bed.
Conway saw Baron Samedi again and again in his dreams.
In the end he went crazy.

William Shakespeare

A Checking your understanding

Chapters 1–3

1 Twelfth Night.
2 He was a glove-maker, but he had other business too, like buying and selling sheep.
3 Eighteen.
4 Susanna, Hamnet and Judith.

Chapters 4–6

1 T   2 F   3 F   4 T   5 T

6 F   7 T   8 F

Chapters 7–9

1 Queen Elizabeth (the First).
2 The Globe theatre.
3 Richard Burbage.
4 James the First.
5 Susanna, Will's daughter.
6 The Mermaid Tavern, in Cheapside, London.
7 Ben Jonson.

Chapters 10–12

1 Because the building had a roof, so they could put on plays in the evenings and in any weather. The Blackfriars also had seats and each person paid a shilling for their seat.
2 There was a fire and it burnt right down to the ground in an hour.
3 To go to a party at the Mermaid Tavern.
4 Fifty-two years old.

B Working with language

Exercise 1

1 Will worked for his father in Henley Street when he left school.
2 A new actor only got six shillings a week and there wasn't work every week.
3 Toby didn't want to be an actor because he couldn't remember his words.
4 Perhaps Emilia Lanier was Will's Dark Lady, but Toby didn't really know.

Exercise 2

1 & 8   2 & 5   3 & 6   4 & 7

The Year of Sharing

A Checking your understanding

Chapter 1

1 T   2 F   3 T   4 F   5 T

Chapter 2

1 Four.
2 Nothing.
3 Because Father stopped him.
4 When the deer swam across a river in the afternoon.
5 Spring.

Chapter 3

1 Because it rained most of the time, and Richard was wet, cold, tired, hungry, and ill, and he missed home.
2 A few wild vegetables and a little fruit.
3 He made some out of leaves.
4 When he decided to stand and fight the wolves.
5 Because he wanted the wolves to think he was afraid; then they would follow him, not Brother.
6 He climbed a tree.

Chapter 4

1 T   2 F   3 F   4 T   5 F

Chapter 5

1 They ran, they swam across water, and they stayed away from soft ground.
2 They followed the strong smell of blood, which was coming from the cut on Baby's leg.
3 Because he wanted to take the wolves away from them.
4 Perhaps he fell off the rocks in his sleep and was killed. Perhaps he fell, hurt himself, and couldn't run, and so the wolves caught him and killed him. Perhaps he died of hunger and cold.

B Working with language

Exercise 1

1 & 10   2 & 8   3 & 9   4 & 6   5 & 7

Exercise 2

6, 3, 10, 5, 8, 1, 4, 2, 7, 9

STAGE THREE

As the Inspector Said . . .

A Checking your understanding

As the Inspector Said . . .

1 The inspector.
2 Robert.

The Man Who Cut Off My Hair

1 She could lip-read.
2 At the Cloakroom, Victoria Station, Brighton Railway.

The Railway Crossing

1 T   2 F

The Blue Cross

1 Father Brown threw soup at it.
2 To leave the parcel and an address for it.

Cash on Delivery

1 From a lonely field in Norfolk.
2 A hand.

B Working with language

As the Inspector Said . . .

1   3   2

The Man Who Cut Off My Hair

1 The other man looked at me while I was watching his friend speak.
2 I knew Myrtle Cottage because it was not very far from our own cottage.
3 The man with the parcel saw us and at once he dropped the parcel and ran off.

The Railway Crossing

1 & 6   2 & 5   3 & 4

The Blue Cross

2   1   3

Cash on Delivery

1 It was not difficult to reach and the window was unlocked as promised.
2 He was not interested in murder if robbery could do the same job.
3 Linster gently put her body on the floor then covered her with a blanket from the bed.

The Brontë Story

A Checking your understanding

Chapters 1–3

1 Patrick Brontë, Mr Nicholls, and their servant.
2 In April 1820.
3 Maria, Elizabeth, Charlotte, and Emily.
4 The food was bad, the school was very cold, and the teachers were unkind.
5 They both died.
6 Because they were given some toy soldiers and began inventing stories about them.
7 Angria and Gondal.

Chapters 4–6

1 F   2 T   3 T   4 F   5 F
6 F   7 T

Chapters 7–8

1 Emily, about some of her poems.
2 Patrick Brontë, about Charlotte's book.
3 Charlotte, about changing the paper on the packet containing her book The Professor which she sent to one publisher after another.
4 Anne, about people who read Charlotte's book *Jane Eyre*.
5 Patrick Brontë, about *Wuthering Heights*.
6 Emily, about a visit from the doctor.

Chapters 9–10

1 Two.
2 Because her book *Jane Eyre* was very popular.
3 Because he paid Mr Nicholls to work for him, not to fall in love with his daughter.
4 Because he was a good husband for Charlotte; he honestly loved her, and could make her happy.
5 Mrs Gaskell.

B Working with language

Exercise 1

1 . . . came to Haworth for the first time.
2 . . . he wanted them to be successful, not poor like his own family.
3 . . . they started playing with the toy soldiers.
4 . . . he came back to Haworth after two weeks.
5 . . . they wanted to live and work together.

6 ... Mr Robinson had ordered him never to return to his house.
7 ... the three sisters used men's names.

Exercise 2

4, 6, 8, 1, 9, 3, 7, 2, 5

Chemical Secret

A Checking your understanding

Chapters 1–2

1 T   2 F   3 T   4 F

Chapters 3–4

1 It was very hard and strong, and nothing could damage it.
2 Because he spilt some of the waste products on his leg and it left a red, painful place on his skin, which kept him awake at night.
3 They were angry with her because she tidied up the kitchen and didn't want to watch TV.
4 Because he saw seals for the first time.

Chapters 5–6

1 For two weeks.
2 Five.
3 Two million pounds.
4 Four hundred.
5 Twice as much.

Chapters 7–8

1 Because she knew the cleaning machines would never be built.
2 Because he always argued with Simon.
3 He had to write an article about the environment every week.
4 They were testing samples of water taken from the river near the sewage works.

Chapters 9–10

1 Simon.
2 David Wilson.
3 Christine.
4 Simon.

Chapters 11–12

1 Because he was in Scotland when the accident happened.
2 He ran out of the room.
3 Because she wouldn't see him or talk to him.
4 Because he was worried that there might be something wrong with the baby.

B Working with language

Exercise 1

6, 3, 8, 10, 7, 2, 5, 9, 4, 1

Exercise 2

1 ... knew he had to.
2 ... people aren't careful with them.'
3 ... we don't put a lot in.'

4 ... he read the newspaper report about Christine's accident.
5 ... your daughter has drunk so much river water?'

Frankenstein

A Checking your understanding

Chapters 1–3

1 T   2 F   3 F   4 T   5 F

Chapters 4–6

1 He got it from lightning.
2 It had a horrible ugly face, with yellow eyes and skin, long black hair and white teeth, and huge arms and legs. It was two and a half metres tall.
3 She thought he had died because she let him wear her gold chain.
4 Because the police had arrested her.
5 Because Victor was his king and creator.
6 Because what the monster said was true.

Chapters 7–9

1 He cut firewood for them.
2 Because he knew they would be frightened by his horrible face and body.
3 He listened to the family talking, and to Felix teaching Sophie.
4 He wanted Felix's father to help him to live with his friends and enjoy their love.
5 The father of the girl who fell in the river shot him, to make him let go of her.
6 He found it around the neck of the child he killed, and he put it in the pocket of a young woman who was asleep in a hut.

Chapters 10–12

1 The monster.
2 Victor.
3 The monster.
4 Henry Clerval.
5 His father.
6 Elizabeth.

Chapters 13–15

1 Because he thought the monster might be there, murdering his father and brother.
2 Because he wanted to kill the monster.
3 Because he wanted him to feel the pain and misery the monster had given him.
4 He wanted him to chase and kill the monster.
5 He made a great fire and lay down on it.

B Working with language

Exercise 1

2 When the sailors woke up in the morning, the ice was floating around the ship.
3 Frankenstein could not walk, so the sailors carried him on to the ship.

4 Frankenstein studied death because he wanted to learn the secret of life.
5 Although Frankenstein wrote to his family less often, they did not stop writing to him.

Exercise 2

Frankenstein searched every corner of the hotel for the monster.

The monster found Elizabeth alone in the room.

Elizabeth screamed.

The monster murdered Elizabeth.

Frankenstein ran back into the room.

The monster watched Frankenstein and Elizabeth through the open window.

Frankenstein fired at the monster.

The monster jumped into the lake.

Frankenstein went with the other people to search for the monster.

Go, Lovely Rose

A Checking your understanding

Go, Lovely Rose

1 Mrs Carteret.
2 Mr Carteret.
3 Nobody.
4 Bill Jordan's mother.
5 Bill Jordan.

The Daffodil Sky

1 Because the footbridge was closed.
2 Eighteen years.
3 He was taking his flowers to the market.
4 Because it kept raining.
5 On the railway.
6 Because they wanted to buy Osborne's farm.
7 Eight hundred pounds.
8 He wanted to ask him if he was the father of Cora's baby.
9 She was working at the shoe factory.
10 Because he was afraid.

The Dam

1 Under the grape vines in the hotel garden.
2 Inside a small wooden building in the forest.
3 At the station in Domodossola.
4 In Munich.
5 To Isola Bella.
6 To Venice.
7 On the dam.

B Working with language

Go, Lovely Rose

1 & 7   2 & 8   3 & 6   4 & 5

The Daffodil Sky

3, 6, 2, 5, 1, 4

The Dam

1 I did a lot of mountain-climbing when I was younger.
2 She always picked some grapes before she began sketching.
3 I get car-sick if I sit in the back.
4 I am Johnson because I prefer my father's name.
5 He kissed her, but his kisses were cold and unnatural.
6 They drank cold white wine and watched the sun on the water.

The Last Sherlock Holmes Story

A Checking your understanding

Foreword and Introduction

1 1976.
2 He was a doctor.
3 A Study in Scarlet.
4 Mary Morstan.

Chapter 1

1 Because he had no interesting cases to think about.
2 The killer cut up the women that he murdered.
3 Some of the policemen would be dressed in women's clothes.
4 'No time to rip'.

Chapter 2

1 T   2 F   3 F   4 T

Chapter 3

1 Run to the police station and fetch Lestrade.
2 He kissed her face.
3 Because he fell asleep. He was asleep for two hours.
4 He was singing.

Chapter 4

1 T   2 T   3 F   4 F

Chapter 5 and Conclusion

1 Because he thought that Moriarty was following him and trying to kill him.
2 A box full of papers about the Whitechapel murders and some glass jars containing pieces of women's bodies.
3 He injected himelf with cocaine.
4 Because he thought that Watson was Moriarty.
5 He stepped off the path above the waterfall and fell to his death on the rocks below.
6 Because he became famous as a story-book detective, in ACD's many successful stories about him.

B Working with language

Exercise 1

1 & 11   2 & 13   3 & 14   4 & 16
5 & 15   6 & 9   7 & 10   8 & 12

Exercise 2

1 . . . he was afraid that Holmes would be there.
2 . . . he picked it up and read it.
3 . . . marry him sooner than they had planned.
4 . . . he was going to work on a murder case in Russia.
5 . . . how Moriarty had died.
6 . . . he was not dead, only resting.

C Activities

Exercise 3

The hidden message in Holmes's letter is:
The professor is alive. He killed Flora White. My letters are read, but I follow him night and day. This time he will not escape.

Love Story

A Checking your understanding

Chapter 1

1 F   2 T   3 F   4 T   5 F

Chapters 2–3

1 Oliver's father, Oliver Barrett the Third.
2 Jenny.
3 Oliver.
4 Jenny.
5 Ray Stratton.
6 Oliver.
7 Jenny.

Chapters 4–5

1 On Hamilton Street, Cranston, Rhode Island.
2 Because he wanted to marry Jenny but he had no money.
3 Because he wanted to get a scholarship for the next year at law school.
4 Four – Jenny, Oliver, Ray, and Phil.
5 An invitation to Oliver's father's sixtieth birthday party.
6 Because Oliver wouldn't accept the invitation and refused even to speak to his father on the telephone; Jenny thought Oliver was heartless and was making his father very unhappy.

Chapters 6–7

1 He came third in his final examinations.
2 Bozo.
3 Because he couldn't leave Jenny.
4 Because they had been too busy buying things for their flat to think about it.
5 Because he wanted to borrow five thousand dollars.
6 He went to live with Oliver in their flat.
7 She asked him to put his arms around her and hold her.

B Working with language

Exercise 1

1 Jenny worked as a teacher while Oliver studied at law school.
2 Although Oliver and Jenny didn't have much money, they were very happy.
3 Oliver and Jenny didn't go out to restaurants because they were too expensive.
4 Their lives changed after Oliver passed his law exams.
5 Oliver and Jenny had no health insurance, so Oliver borrowed money from his father.

Exercise 2

3, 1, 8, 6, 2, 5, 7, 4

The Picture of Dorian Gray

A Checking your understanding

Chapters 1–5

1 Because he felt that he had put too much of himself into it, and that it showed the secret of his heart.
2 Because he was afraid that Lord Henry would change Dorian and take him away from Basil.
3 Youth.
4 He wished that he could always stay young and that the picture could grow old.
5 Because he wanted to listen to him talking.

Chapters 6–10

1 About seventeen.
2 To Australia.
3 Because she had lost her art and wasn't a wonderful actress any more.
4 The mouth had become cruel and unkind.
5 She killed herself.
6 Lord Henry.
7 Because he didn't want anyone else to see the changes in the painting.

Chapters 11–13

1 T   2 F   3 T   4 T   5 F   6 F

Chapters 14–17

1 Because Dorian had destroyed his sister's life.
2 He showed him his face, and James thought he was too young to be his sister's killer.
3 James Vane's.
4 He was shot in an accident.
5 Because he felt he had done too many terrible things in his life.
6 He wanted to know how he had kept his youth and beauty.
7 Because it had stolen every chance of peace or happiness from him.
8 They found a portrait of Dorian Gray, looking young and beautiful, and an ugly old man lying dead on the floor.

B Working with language

Exercise 1

1 I'm not happy if I don't see Dorian every day.
2 Your clever words are very amusing, but you laugh at serious things.
3 Lord Henry talked to Dorian while Basil painted.
4 Every night I see her in different plays and she's always wonderful.
5 Dorian went to see Sybil after the play ended.
6 Sybil killed herself because she loved Dorian.

Exercise 2

3, 5, 2, 8, 7, 10, 1, 9, 4, 6

Skyjack!

A Checking your understanding

Exercise 1

1 Because they wanted the government to set two of their brothers free.
2 Because he didn't want the hijackers to know that Carl was the Prime Minister's husband.
3 They wanted the government to set their two brothers free. Then they wanted the plane to be refuelled. They also wanted a message to be put in all the newspapers.
4 Because they said he was a spy.
5 She disliked the American Ambassador's loud voice and hairy chest. She disliked the British Ambassador because he had once lied to her. And she disliked them both because they were military men who wanted bases for their soldiers in her country.
6 Because one of the raincoat's buttons was a small radio transmitter, and so they could listen to the terrorists talking on the plane.

Exercise 2

Last night, a plane carrying 108 passengers was hijacked. (T)
The Prime Minister's husband, Carl Sandberg, was one of the passengers. (T)
Mr Sandberg was travelling alone. (F)
There were three hijackers, one man and two women. (F)
The hijackers asked the government to set two of their brothers free from prison. (T)
Their brothers were in prison because they had tried to put a bomb on a plane last year. (T)
The hijackers shot an American businessman because he tried to escape from the plane. (F)
After the businessman was shot, Mrs Sandberg agreed to bring the two prisoners to the airport. (T)
Before the prisoners arrived at the airport, the hijackers set free most of the passengers. (F)
Mrs Sandberg sent both of the prisoners on to the plane. (F)
When the first prisoner went on to the plane, he had a small radio transmitter in his coat pocket. (F)
The plane was attacked by soldiers and all of the hijackers were killed. (T)
Luckily, none of the hijackers knew that Mr Sandberg was on the plane. (F)

B Working with language

Exercise 1

4, 10, 11, 5, 2, 9, 3, 7, 12, 13, 8, 1, 6

Model answer
Carl and Harald got onto the plane, and the air hostess helped them to find their seats. After a while Carl lay back in his seat and went to sleep. About midnight he woke up and asked the air hostess for a cup of coffee. Then he started to read his newspaper. A little later Carl showed Harald a photo in the newspaper. Harald smiled at it and put the newspaper in his coat pocket. Then he called for the air hostess, but she didn't come. When he looked for her, he saw her talking with two young men.

The Star Zoo

A Checking your understanding

Chapters 1–3
1 T   2 F   3 F   4 T   5 T
6 F   7 F   8 T

Chapters 4–6
1 Cheep-Cheep.
2 Hoo-Woo and Hee-Haw.
3 The computer.
4 Hummy.
5 Hummy's father.
6 Buff.

Chapters 7–8
1 Warm wet plastic came out of a pipe in the wall and the squirrel ran up and down carrying bits of the soft plastic to cover the hole.
2 He went crazy when he saw the animals.
3 Because Hummy thought that although the computer was twenty thousand years old, it was still young, like her, and was still growing and changing.
4 The computer's idea was that humans should learn about animals from robot animals. Then later humans would not be afraid when they met real animals.
5 She chose the animal that liked playing with humans.
6 Inside its stomach.

Chapters 9–10
1 On New Earth.
2 They took him to hospital.
3 She was afraid they would go crazy.
4 An official shot it with his laser gun.

5 Because it was the only way to keep the Star Zoo alive.
6 Her job was to take care of some little children.
7 Because they had never heard of Earth or the Book of Remembering.
8 Her plan was to have a special room in each house which parents couldn't go in and where children could play with robot animals. Then the children would still be happy to be with animals when they were parents.

B Working with language

Exercise 1
4, 7, 2, 6, 3, 1, 5

Exercise 2
1 & 9   2 & 7   3 & 10   4 & 6   5 & 8

Tales of Mystery and Imagination

A Checking your understanding

The Fall of the House of Usher
1 F   2 F   3 T   4 T   5 F

The Black Cat
1 Because he thought animals were more friendly and more honest than most men.
2 He found a rope, tied it round Pluto's neck, and hung him from a tree.
3 It had a white mark on its front.
4 Because he became angry when she tried to stop him killing the second cat.
5 Because the narrator knocked on the wall with a stick to show how strong it was. Then the cat, which he had put into the wall with his dead wife, began to scream loudly.

The Masque of the Red Death
1 Half the people.
2 A thousand.
3 Blue, purple, green, orange, white, violet, and black with red windows.
4 At midnight.
5 Nothing.

William Wilson
1 He never spoke above a whisper.
2 Because, when he looked at William Wilson asleep, he was more frightened than he had ever been in his life.
3 Because he was known to be a cheat at cards and every door in England was closed against him.
4 They were always the same clothes as the narrator was wearing.
5 The narrator's conscience (the part of him that was honest and good, and that told him not to do evil things).

The Tell-Tale Heart
1 F   2 T   3 T   4 F   5 F

B Working with language

The Fall of the House of Usher
1 & 8   2 & 6   3 & 5   4 & 7

William Wilson
1 . . . liked to give orders, not to take them.
2 . . . win money from the other students and become even richer.
3 . . . helped me to win every game I played.
4 . . . I escaped to Europe, but everywhere I went, William Wilson appeared like a ghost and came between me and my plans.
5 . . . I saw myself, walking forward shakily, my face white, and covered with blood.

Tooth and Claw

A Checking your understanding

Sredni Vashtar
1 An old, untidy-looking chicken.
2 His aunt sold it.
3 Because his aunt said that it was bad for him.
4 In Conradin's bedroom.
5 It killed his aunt.

The Story-Teller
1 They thought it was stupid.
2 Because she was so good.
3 Because once in a dream the king's mother heard a voice say, 'Your son will be killed by a sheep.'
4 Because the pigs had eaten them all.
5 It heard her medals clinking.
6 They thought it was the most beautiful story they had ever heard.

Gabriel-Ernest
1 F   2 T   3 F   4 F   5 T

Tobermory
1 Clovis.
2 Sir Wilfrid.
3 Major Barfield.
4 Agnes Resker.
5 Sir Wilfrid.
6 Cornelius Appin.

The She-Wolf
1 Because he wanted to do his own 'Siberian Magic' and to pretend to change Mary Hampton into a wolf.
2 She disappeared behind a plant and then a big grey wolf came out.
3 He gave her some sugar, and she followed him out of the room hoping for more.
4 Because Clovis made him look very silly.

B Working with language

Gabriel-Ernest
1 . . . while he was walking in the woods.

2 ... so he went to see Cunningham in London.
3 ... because he said Van Cheele would think he was crazy.
4 ... but he was too late to save Jack.
5 Although Van Cheele usually did what his aunt wanted, he refused to give any money for Gabriel-Ernest's memorial.

The She-Wolf

5, 3, 7, 6, 9, 1, 8, 2, 4

Wyatt's Hurricane

A Checking your understanding

Chapters 1–3
1 F   2 T   3 F   4 T   5 T   6 F
7 T

Chapters 4–6
1 More than fifteen metres.
2 Causton.
3 In 1910.
4 He told her to stay with Mr Rawsthorne and Mrs Warmington and find a place to hide in the hotel.
5 He hid in an empty shop.
6 They made a hole in the wall and crawled out.
7 Because Causton had told him about Wyatt and hurricane Mabel.
8 Sixty thousand.
9 Because he didn't want to take a chance with the lives of his people.

Chapters 7–10
1 He wanted to get all the people out of St Pierre and let Serrurier and his army take the city.
2 Because he didn't want Favel to use the hurricane as a weapon.
3 Serrurier had fifteen thousand men and Favel had five thousand.
4 Because the people of St Pierre were now moving up the Negrito valley, so she knew Wyatt had warned them about the hurricane.
5 More than 250 kilometres an hour.
6 St Pierre had disappeared under the sea.
7 Because there was a report about some foreigners up the Negrito valley, and Wyatt thought Julie might be there.
8 They were trapped under a tree.
9 Captain Brooks and some doctors.
10 He felt he hadn't done his job as a weatherman very well because too many people had died.

B Working with language

Exercise 1
1 ... get information about it.
2 ... Schelling didn't agree with him.
3 ... he had heard that Favel was still alive.
4 ... they saw an old man getting his house ready for the hurricane.

5 ... thousands of people will die in St Pierre.
6 ... he wouldn't listen to him.

Exercise 2
4 & 8   6 & 1   10 & 3 & 9   5 & 11   2 & 7

The Big Sleep

A Checking your understanding

Chapters 1–3
1 Because he wanted Marlowe to get rid of Arthur Geiger for him.
2 He had disappeared a month earlier.
3 They made their money from oil.
4 It appeared to be a specialist bookshop.
5 It was a library where people could borrow pornographic books.
6 A pair of long green ear-rings.

Chapters 4–6
1 F   2 T   3 F   4 T   5 T

Chapters 7–9
1 Carol Lundgren.
2 In Carol's room at Geiger's house.
3 Because he didn't want his clients' names to appear in the newspaper reports of the murders.
4 Because he wanted to find out what had happened to Rusty Regan.
5 Five hundred dollars.
6 To the Cypress Club.

Chapters 10–12
1 She played roulette.
2 Eddie Mars took it back from her.
3 Carmen Sternwood.
4 Because he wanted to sell him some information about Rusty Regan.
5 Canino put cyanide in his whisky.
6 Agnes.

Chapters 13–15
1 F   2 T   3 F   4 T   5 T
6 F   7 T

B Working with language

Exercise 1
1 ... he was very fond of him, but Regan disappeared without saying goodbye.
2 ... she knew nothing about them.
3 ... gave him back his job as their chauffeur.
4 ... he shot Brody.
5 ... he loved Carmen, and he didn't like what Geiger was doing with her.

Exercise 2

1 After Marlowe heard Harry Jones's story, he agreed to pay 200 dollars.
2 Canino killed Harry Jones while Marlow was listening behind a door.
3 Marlowe didn't realize what was happening until it was too late.
4 Harry had given Canino Agnes's address, but it was a false one.
5 Agnes recognized Mona Mars when she saw her in a car with Canino.
6 Mona Mars wanted to help Eddie because she loved him.

Death of an Englishman

A Checking your understanding

Chapters 1–3

1 Because the Marshal was in bed with a cold upstairs in his flat.
2 Because he thought it might not be an important call.
3 He was sitting up straight in an armchair.
4 Because the dead man belonged to quite an important English family.
5 It was the sound of the big front door closing.

Chapters 4–6

1 F   2 T   3 F   4 T   5 F

Chapters 7–9

1 He had a key to the flat door.
2 None.
3 He was at the funeral of Cipolla's wife.
4 Because Giovanna's school had closed for Christmas, so she wasn't coming home with Martha as usual.
5 Because the window in the lift door was small and high, so he couldn't see if there was anyone bending down inside the lift.

Chapters 10–11

1 He picked it up and put it in a black rubbish bag, and then put the bag in the entrance hall next to the lift.
2 Because he was a sad little man whose life was hard.
3 He had a difficult life. His family was poor, they had little food, and he hated living in the country.
4 Because they needed the money to pay for her funeral.
5 He said that Cesarini had arranged for her to clean the flat, so Cesarini would have to pay her.
6 Because he wanted to make the Englishman listen to him.
7 He told him to keep his eyes on the details of real life, and to ask an officer with more experience if he didn't know what to do.

B Working with language

Exercise 1

1 . . . because he had been shot in the back.
2 . . . although the safe was open.
3 . . . if the visitor was holding a gun.
4 . . . until he fell asleep.
5 . . . but she didn't get up.

Exercise 2

1 & 4   2 & 6   3 & 10   5 & 8   9 & 7

Desert, Mountain, Sea

A Checking your understanding

Across the Australian Desert

1 F   2 F   3 T   4 F   5 T

Climbing Annapurna

1 They organised dances, sports, and parties, and sold expedition T-shirts.
2 In the Himalayas in 1976.
3 Alison Chadwick and Liz Klobusicky.
4 Because they wanted more money and better equipment.
5 They fell 500 metres down the mountain on their way to Camp 5.

Alone around the World

1 She was a hairdresser.
2 In St Malo in France on the yacht British Steel.
3 In her parents' living-room in New Zealand.
4 Because her Sailomat and her radio needed repairing.
5 Dartmouth.

B Working with language

Across the Australian Desert

2, 6, 1, 3, 9, 7, 4, 8, 5

Climbing Annapurna

1 Arlene Blum had the idea of climbing Annapurna when she was in the Himalayas.
2 Annapurna is a very dangerous mountain because it has avalanches at any time of the day or night.
3 Vera Watson and Alison Chadwick decided to try to climb to the summit although they did not have enough oxygen.
4 Arlene was very worried about the two women so she sent the Sherpas to look for them.
5 The Sherpas found the women's bodies on the mountain after they had searched for many hours.

Alone around the World

1 & 8   2 & 10   3 & 7   4 & 6   5 & 9

Dr Jekyll and Mr Hyde

A Checking your understanding

Chapters 1–2
1 T   2 F   3 F   4 T   5 T   6 F

Chapters 3–4
1 Mr Hyde's servant.
2 The police inspector.
3 The servant girl, who saw Mr Hyde murder Sir Danvers Carew.
4 Dr Jekyll.
5 Mr Utterson.
6 Mr Guest, Mr Utterson's chief clerk.

Chapters 5–7
1 All their lives.
2 To the laboratory at the back of Dr Jekyll's house.
3 Mr Utterson.
4 He thought someone had murdered him.
5 He took poison.
6 A packet with three envelopes inside, containing Dr Jekyll's will, a short note from him to Mr Utterson, and his confessions.

Chapters 8–9
1 He asked him to fetch some chemical powders, a bottle, and a book from his house and give them to a man who would come at midnight.
2 As a doctor he felt sorry for him, but as a man he felt only fear and dislike.
3 Because he could no longer sleep and he felt filled with fear and horror all the time.
4 Because he wanted both sides of his character to be free to do what they wanted.
5 He felt young and carefree.
6 Jekyll was mostly good, kind, and honest, but Hyde was pure evil.
7 When he woke up one morning and found that he was Edward Hyde, even though he had gone to bed as Henry Jekyll.
8 Because he could no longer stop himself changing into Hyde and knew he would soon lose Jekyll's face and character for ever – and if anyone saw him as Hyde, he would be arrested for murder.
9 Because he couldn't find more chemicals that were exactly like the ones he had used before.

B Working with language

Exercise 1
1 . . . because he knew it already.
2 . . . after Dr Jekyll died.
3 . . . because it was a stick that he had given to Dr Jekyll long ago.
4 . . . but they couldn't get a photograph or a good description of him.
5 . . . until Dr Jekyll died or disappeared.
6 Although Mr Utterson visited Dr Jekyll every day, Jekyll always refused to see him.

Exercise 2
3 & 6   9 & 2   10 & 12 & 8 & 4
11 & 5 & 1 & 7

The Hound of the Baskervilles

A Checking your understanding

Chapters 1–4
1 On the night in 1640 when Hugo Baskerville died.
2 In the first part of Yew Alley there were whole footprints, but after the moor gate the prints were only of Sir Charles' toes.
3 Dr Mortimer.
4 Because he found two lots of ash which had dropped off the end of Sir Charles' cigar.

Chapters 5–9
1 F   2 T   3 T   4 F   5 T

Chapters 10–14
1 Laura Lyons.
2 He saw a young boy going onto the moor each day with a bag on his shoulder.
3 Because he wanted to make sure that Watson and Sir Henry were safe, but he didn't want the enemy to know he was there.
4 Because he was wearing Sir Henry's suit.

Chapters 15–18
1 Stapleton.
2 Because he wanted Stapleton to think that Holmes and Watson had gone away.
3 He told her he loved her and wanted to marry her.
4 Because it seemed to be covered in flames, because of the phosphorus paint.
5 To stop her from helping Sir Henry.
6 He lost his way in the fog and sank to his death in the marsh.
7 Because then he would inherit the Baskerville lands and fortune.

B Working with language

Exercise 1
1 . . . because he needed his help and advice.
2 Because Dr Mortimer was a man of science, he believed that there were sensible explanations for everything.
3 . . . after his new shoe was stolen.
4 . . . if he went on the moor at night.
5 . . . since he was working on another case.

Exercise 2
3 & 6 & 8 & 11   4 & 1   10 & 5
12 & 9   7 & 2

Mr Midshipman Hornblower

A Checking your understanding

The Even Chance

1 T 2 F 3 F 4 T 5 T 6 F

The Cargo of Rice

1 To sail her to England and wait there for orders.
2 Because the rice in the hold had taken in the water.
3 Because the cargo of rice got bigger and bigger and made cracks between the boards of the ship until at last the ship sank.
4 Because he didn't think they could all survive in the small boat for a week.
5 He pulled pages out of his book and lit the paper with his lamp.
6 Because the French captain had to turn his ship around and sail towards the *Indefatigable* in order to stop the wind blowing the flames through the ship.

The Spanish Galleys

1 The galley slaves.
2 The English in Gibraltar.
3 Jackson.
4 Hornblower.
5 Jackson and Oldroyd.
6 Oldroyd.

The Duchess and the Devil

1 He was taking *Le Rêve* to England, carrying the Admiral's despatches.
2 Because there was a thick fog.
3 He gave them to the duchess and she hid them under her dress.
4 Because he had been promoted to lieutenant.
5 Because he had promised not to break parole and try to escape.
6 Because he had saved the lives of the Spanish sailors.

B Working with language

The Even Chance

1 Simpson had been sent to another ship to work as a lieutenant, but he had failed his examination, and he was now a midshipman again.
2 The other midshipmen were very surprised when Simpson came back to the *Justinian* and took his seat at the head of the table.
3 Simpson was not very clever, but he knew how to find out people's weaknesses.
4 Several other midshipmen tried to fight Simpson, but nobody managed to beat him.
5 Simpson was unhurt, while Lieutenant Masters noticed the loser's bruises and punished him instead of Simpson.

The Duchess and the Devil

1 . . . because she had only four small guns.

2 . . . before he could see them.
3 . . . until she could give them to a King's officer.
4 Although Hornblower tried to escape from the Spanish fleet, the Spanish ships were all around them and escape was impossible.
5 . . . so she pretended to be a duchess.
6 Because Hornblower had given his parole to the Spanish, he decided not to stay on the *Syrtis*.
7 . . . as soon as the storm was over.

The Moonspinners

A Checking your understanding

Chapters 1–4

1 F 2 T 3 T 4 F

Chapters 5–9

1 Because they wanted to be able to see anyone who came looking for Mark.
2 To fetch some food and to see if Colin was there.
3 Nicola's cousin told him when she phoned.
4 At Sofia's house.
5 She told her to keep away from trouble.
6 To see if Colin was there.

Chapters 10–12

1 She saw some pieces of bread, a rope with blood on it, and a piece of material that had been in Colin's mouth.
2 She saw a spade and remembered a man digging in a field near the windmill, so she thought he had buried Colin's body.
3 A sheep's coat.
4 Sofia.
5 Because he wanted to make Lambis tell them what had happened to Mark.
6 Because he was wearing Josef's clothes.

Chapters 13–16

1 F 2 T 3 T 4 T 5 F 6 F

B Working with language

Exercise 1

7, 4, 6, 1, 10, 3, 5, 9, 2, 8

Exercise 2

1 The hotel was not expecting me, so I decided to stay by the river and eat my lunch.
2 I wanted to know where the boat was in case I needed help myself.
3 Although Sofia was poor, she would not take money from her brother.
4 When I returned to the hotel, Stratos came with me.
5 Nicola wanted to go to the windmill because she thought Colin was there.
6 Nicola thought she was safe until she found Josef's knife in her pocket.

Reflex

A Checking your understanding

Chapters 1–2
1 Photography.
2 Six.
3 Because Steve had hurt his shoulder.
4 He went to sleep while driving his car and crashed it.
5 In the fridge.

Chapters 3–5
1 F   2 T   3 T   4 F   5 T

Chapters 6–8
1 . . . cookery.
2 . . . photographs.
3 George . . . .
4 . . . Hong Kong.

Chapters 9–11
1 T   2 F   3 T   4 T   5 F

Chapters 12–14
1 A gun.
2 Some champagne.
3 Salt.
4 Paper for printing photographs.
5 Plastic.

Chapters 15–16
1 *Open answer.*
2 *Open answer.*

B Working with language

Exercise 1
1 & 8   2 & 6   3 & 5   4 & 7

Exercise 2
Just then there was a heavy crash from downstairs. Philip and Clare found Jeremy face down on the floor. There was a strong smell of bad eggs, so Philip pushed Clare outside the front door. Next, he pulled Jeremy through the hall to the front door. Meanwhile, Clare had called a neighbour and the ambulance. The neighbour breathed into Jeremy, but Jeremy didn't move. As soon as the ambulance arrived, it took Jeremy to hospital.

Silas Marner

A Checking your understanding

Chapters 1–2
1 Because they thought Silas's way of life was very strange, and they believed that he had an almost devilish power.
2 From a large town to the north of Raveloe.
3 Because he was (wrongly) accused of stealing money.
4 His 'friend', William Dane.
5 He was secretly married to Molly, a poor girl from the town.
6 To sell it for Godfrey, so that Godfrey could give the money back to the Squire.
7 Because the doorkey was holding Silas's piece of meat in place over the fire.

Chapters 3–4
1 F   2 T   3 F   4 F   5 T   6 F

Chapters 5–7
1 Old Mr Macey, the church clerk, and Dolly Winthrop with her little son Aaron.
2 The New Year's Eve dance which Squire Cass gave at the Red House.
3 Nancy Lammeter.
4 The soft, warm, golden curls of the sleeping child.
5 Only one – Godfrey Cass.
6 Eppie, because that had been his little sister's name.

Chapters 8–10
1 The death of her only baby, and the fact that she could have no more children.
2 She told him that she and Aaron Winthrop wanted to get married.
3 The dead body of Dunstan Cass, with Silas's bags of gold.
4 Because he thought that everybody's secrets were discovered sooner or later, and he didn't want Nancy to discover it from someone else or to hear about it when he was dead.
5 Because she loved Silas and wanted to stay with him.

B Working with language

Exercise 1
1 . . . he loved them and thought they were his friends, who made the cottage less lonely for him.
2 . . . Godfrey told him that he had given Fowler's money to Dunstan and so could not repay the Squire.
3 . . . Silas did not go and spent the day alone in his cottage.
4 . . . his first wife, Molly, died.
5 . . . he adopted Eppie as his child.

Exercise 2
3, 1, 5, 8, 2, 7, 6, 4

The Thirty-Nine Steps

A Checking your understanding

Chapters 1–2
1 In Africa.
2 American.
3 With a knife through his heart.
4 He disguised himself as a milkman.
5 To Galloway in Scotland.

Chapters 3–4

1 T   2 F   3 F   4 T   5 T

Chapters 5–6

1 Because he had been dancing and drinking at his daughter's wedding until four o'clock in the morning.
2 He borrowed the roadman's hat, glasses, and pipe. He put dirt on his face, hands, and clothes, and rubbed some into his eyes to make them red. He also kicked his boots against the rocks to make them look older.
3 Because, although he knew Hannay's name, he had never seen him before.
4 He used explosives to blow up the room where he was locked in.
5 He hid on the roof of an old tower.

Chapters 7–8

1 T   2 F   3 T   4 F   5 F

Chapters 9–10

1 MacGillivray.
2 Hannay.
3 A servant.
4 The fat man.
5 The thin man.

B Working with language

Exercise 1

1 & 10 2 & 7 3 & 8 4 & 6 5 & 9

Exercise 2

Hannay went to Trafalgar House, although he wasn't sure that the men who lived there were the spies. When he told them he was arresting them, they were very surprised. While they were waiting for Hannay to decide, they played cards. At ten o'clock, Hannay decided that the men were the spies, and blew his whistle. As soon as he heard the whistle, the thin man ran away.

Three Men in a Boat

A Checking your understanding

Chapters 1–4

1 F   2 F   3 T   4 F   5 T   6 T

Chapters 5–8

1 He read them interesting pieces from the newspaper – pieces about people who had been killed on the river, and interesting reports about the weather.
2 One of the old keepers came and let them out.
3 Harris.
4 Because he'd had a bad day at the bank.
5 George.

Chapters 9–12

1 Because they had told him to stand and wait.
2 While he was climbing along the branch of a tree the branch broke and he fell into the river.
3 George's.
4 Because there were no roses round the door, and J. wanted somewhere with roses round the door.
5 Because they could not open the tin.
6 Because the cat frightened him.
7 He told them to drink water from the river.

Chapters 13–16

1 He drank a lot of whisky.
2 He likes it and thinks it is very interesting. He can sit and look at it for hours.
3 Because they were so dirty.
4 Five.
5 George.
6 Because they thought it would be more interesting to go to a theatre and a restaurant in London than to stay in Pangbourne in the rain.

B Working with language

Exercise 1

3, 5, 8, 1, 7, 4, 6, 2

Exercise 2

1 . . . it looked too wet and cold.
2 . . . he climbed onto the branch of a tree which was over the water.
3 . . . fell into the river.
4 . . . started to laugh.
5 . . . noticed that it was not his.

Exercise 3

After that, we could think of nothing else to do, so we went to bed. Well, we undressed and we lay down in the boat. We tried to go to sleep, but it was four hours before we did so. At five o'clock we all woke up again, so we got up and had breakfast.

Brat Farrar

A Checking your understanding

Chapters 1–4

1 T   2 F   3 T   4 T   5 F

Chapters 5–8

1 Because Simon was a child when his brother died.
2 Because he was worried about doing something criminal.
3 He had to show that he knew the way to the old nursery.
4 He was puzzled that Simon had been very afraid at first, and then very relieved.
5 He remembered the little wooden horse called

Travesty – the toy which used to hang at the end of Patrick's bed.
6 Simon's.

Chapters 9–12
1 Peggy Gates.
2 Old Felix, the Master of the Hunt.
3 Simon.
4 Brat.
5 Jane.
6 Simon.
7 Roger Clint.

Chapters 12–16
1 Because he knew that Brat could never tell anyone.
2 Because he couldn't decide what to do, and he wanted George's advice.
3 So that he could climb down the rope into the quarry.
4 He went to the quarry first and waited for Brat.
5 He lay on top of the rope.
6 That the body in the quarry was Patrick's.
7 Eleanor kissed him.
8 Because she wanted to have a life of her own away from Latchetts and she knew Uncle Charles would look after it now, and also because she wanted to offer Brat a new home and job.

B Working with language

Exercise 1
4, 7, 10, 5, 1, 3, 9, 2, 8, 6

Brat bought a long piece of rope, then at night he made footholds at regular intervals along it. He went very quietly to Tanbitches, and on the way he listened carefully but heard nothing. After Brat tied the rope round one of the trees, he slid over the edge of the cliff. Meanwhile, Simon was waiting for Brat at Tanbitches, because he planned to cut the rope and let Brat fall to his death. But when Brat caught hold of both Simon's wrists, Simon fell on top of Brat, and they both fell into the quarry.

Exercise 2
1 . . . after he and his wife died in a plane crash.
2 Although he didn't like Loding's plan, Brat decided to go and look at his photographs.
3 . . . so that the horse might try to kill him.
4 . . . unless Brat could prove Simon had killed Patrick.
5 If Brat was killed, Simon would be safe.

The Bride Price

A Checking your understanding

Chapters 1–3
1 F   2 T   3 F   4 T

Chapters 4–6
1 Because it was their home town, where their father's brother and his family lived.
2 She was afraid that she might not be able to stay at school, and that she might have to marry a farmer.
3 He wanted the money in order to become an Obi.
4 He wanted him to leave Ibuza and go to university.
5 Because Chike came from a 'slave' family, and no daughter of a free family was allowed to marry a slave.

Chapters 7–10
1 At a quiet place by the river.
2 He bought them and threw them away so that Aku-nna could stay and talk to him instead of going to the market.
3 Chike.
4 They went to congratulate Aku-nna's family because she had passed her examination.
5 Okoboshi's family.

Chapters 11–13
1 She was worried that she would die in childbirth if it was not paid.
2 Because he thought that Aku-nna was the cause of all his troubles and he wanted her to die.
3 He thought that the doll would not harm her if she knew nothing about it.
4 *Open answer.*

B Working with language

Exercise 1
which, and, before, so that, on the other hand, Although, and. therefore, who

Exercise 2
Model answer
When Aku-nna and Chike ran away from Ibuza and got married, everyone spoke against Chike and his family. Chike's father tried to pay the bride price, but Okonkwo, who was Aku-nna's uncle, refused to accept it because Chike came from a 'slave' family. Although Aku-nna was very happy with Chike, she became more and more worried because her family would not recognize her marriage. Aku-nna knew that the bride price had to be paid.

David Copperfield

A Checking your understanding

Chapters 1–2
1 Clara.
2 Yarmouth.
3 Five days and nights.
4 Eight shillings.
5 'Barkis is willing.'
6 Mr Mell.

    7 Salem House.
    8 Mr Creakle.
    9 Tommy Traddles.
  10 His mother had a new baby.

Chapters 3–5

1 F	2 F	3 T	4 F	5 T
6 F	7 T	8 F		

B Working with language

Exercise 1

6 & 4 & 1   11 & 9   5 & 12   3 & 7 & 10   2 & 8

Model answer
When Uriah Heep came to David's rooms for coffee,
he explained to David that he wanted to marry
Agnes one day. One day David was invited to Mr
Spenlow's house, and immediately fell in love with
Dora Spenlow. Soon afterwards David met Tommy
Traddles and the Micawbers, who were delighted to
see him again. David returned to Yarmouth in order
to help his old friend Peggotty, whose husband,
Barkis, was dying. The day after Barkis's funeral
Ham brought the terrible news that Emily had run
away with Steerforth.

Exercise 2

1 & 12   2 & 9   3 & 11   4 & 7   5 & 8   6 & 10

The Dead of Jericho

A Checking your understanding

Chapters 1–4

1 T	2 F	3 F	4 F	5 T	6 T

Chapters 5–9

1 He bought one from the locksmith in Walton
  Street.
2 £1000.
3 A book by Sophocles.
4 Summertown Bridge Club and Oxford Book
  Club.
5 He said Anne had told him the week before that
  she couldn't give him a lesson on the 3rd.
6 Because he thought that Charles Richards had
  killed him before he went to the Oxford Book
  Club at 8 p.m.
7 Because he thought he was the best man to solve
  the case.
8 She went to get the letters that her husband had
  written to Anne.

Chapters 10–14

1 In the shed in his garden.
2 The Jericho Testing Laboratory.
3 Michael and Edward Murdoch.
4 Charles Richards.
5 Conrad Richards.
6 Charles Richards.

B Working with language

Exercise 1

1 Because the phone box smelt of fish, it must have
  been Jackson who phoned the police to tell them
  Anne was dead.
2 . . . in case she lost hers.
3 . . . as he couldn't read.
4 . . . as soon as he remembered it.
5 . . . since she was expecting someone to fit her
  new curtains.

Exercise 2

Model answer
A young man called Oedipus visited a strange town
and fell in love with the beautiful Queen Jocasta,
who lived there. Her husband the king had died
recently so she and Oedipus married and had several
children. When Oedipus discovered that Jocasta was
his mother, she became desperate and hanged
herself. Oedipus blamed himself for her death, so he
blinded himself.

Far from the Madding Crowd

A Checking your understanding

Chapters 1–5

1 On Norcombe Hill, in Dorset.
2 Twopence.
3 Mrs Hurst.
4 Two hundred.
5 Any two of Billy Smallbury, Joseph Poorgrass,
  and Jan Coggan.
6 Fanny Robin.
7 Marry me.

Chapters 6–9

1 F	2 F	3 T	4 F	5 T	6 F
7 F	8 T				

Chapters 10–19

1 Because he had never seen him there.
2 Because she wanted to see Troy so he could help
  her decide what to do.
3 Because he wanted to make Troy marry Fanny
  Robin and prevent him from marrying
  Bathsheba.
4 Because Troy's brandy had made them all drunk
  and they were all asleep.
5 She died because she was too ill and weak to live
  after her baby was born.

B Working with language

Exercise 1

1 . . . he received Bathsheba's valentine.
2 . . . she had asked him not to tell anyone about
  her marriage.
3 . . . trust Sergeant Troy.
4 . . . put on horses.
5 . . . she was very tired and ill.

Exercise 2

1 & f   2 & d   3 & b   4 & a   5 & c   6 & e

Ghost Stories

A Checking your understanding

Smee
1 Jackson.
2 Brenda Ford.
3 Reggie Sangston.
4 Jack Sangston.

The Judge's House
1 Mr Carnford.
2 Mrs Wood.
3 Mrs Dempster.
4 John Moore.
5 The rats.
6 The people of Benchurch.

The Stranger in the Mist
1 So that he could study the rocks he found.
2 It was built after the map was made.
3 If they followed the map, they could fall off the cliff and kill themselves.

The Confession of Charles Linkworth
1 Linkworth's spirit spoke to him on the telephone.
2 It made a cold wind blow in the room although the window was closed.
3 It disappeared with Linkworth's ghost when the chaplain said the words of forgiveness.

The Ghost Coach
1 James Murray.
2 *Name not given.*
3 Jacob.
4 *Name not given.*
5 King.
6 *Name not given.*

Fullcircle
The Giffens made the chapel into a workroom.
The Giffens invited serious but boring visitors to stay.
The Giffens bought a picture of the first owner of Fullcircle.
Mrs Giffen became a Catholic and Mr Giffen decided to do the same.

B Working with language

The Stranger in the Mist
1 ... the part of Wales where Beverley lived is very interesting to geologists.
2 ... a thick damp mist covered everything.
3 ... came down to his ankles.
4 ... the old man had shown him.
5 ... give to travellers who had lost their way.

The Ghost Coach
I wanted to shake his hand, but he had already turned away.
Although the wind was quieter, it was still bitterly cold.
Although it was dark, I could still see the stone wall at the edge of the road.
I repeated my question more loudly, but he still did not answer.

Great Expectations

A Checking your understanding

Chapters 1–6
1 Some bread, some cheese, and a big meat pie.
2 Mrs Joe Gargery.
3 Mrs Joe's strongest and most unpleasant medicine.
4 Miss Havisham.
5 Twenty-five pounds.
6 Orlick.

Chapters 7–12
1 T   2 F   3 F   4 T   5 T

Chapters 13–19
1 Compeyson.
2 Because he wanted to continue paying Clarrikers but he didn't want to use Magwitch's money any more.
3 Abel Magwitch and Mr Jagger's housekeeper.
4 Orlick, because he hated Pip.
5 He fell into the river and drowned.
6 Because she had married Joe.

B Working with language

Exercise 1
1 ... until she went to the kitchen to get it during the Christmas lunch next day.
2 ... after Pipe learned about his great expectations.
3 ... although he knew she would never love him.
4 ... unless he left the country.

Exercise 2
2 & 8   1 & 10   3 & 6   7 & 9   12 & 5   4 & 11

Heat and Dust

A Checking your understanding

Introduction
1 Her grandfather.
2 In September 1923.
3 In 1923.
4 Olivia's sister Marcia.
5 In February 1973.

The diary

1 He had been studying the Hindu religion and travelling across India.
2 She was a holy woman, a friend of Inder Lal's mother.
3 She was mentally ill.
4 Because he felt ashamed of being poor and felt that she laughed at India and the Indians.
5 Because she felt that he didn't enjoy having a family.
6 To a small town up in the mountains.

The 1923 story

1 Because she had an elegant dress to wear and she wanted to meet new people.
2 To go and stay in Simla in the hills.
3 Because he wanted to see his mother.
4 There was fighting between Muslims and Hindus, and six people were killed and forty-three injured.
5 She said she went to visit Harry, who was ill.
6 Six years.

Discussion

Open answers.

B Working with language

Exercise 1

1 . . . before she told Douglas.
2 . . . as there was no ambulance to bring her to the hospital.
3 Although Chid was very interested in Indian religion, he began to hate India and wanted to go home.
4 . . . in order to become pregnant.
5 . . . unless she had changed, like Olivia.

Exercise 2

Although Harry was very fond of the Nawab, he wanted to go home to England because his mother was ill and lived alone. Mrs Crawford arranged for her friends to drive Harry to Bombay to catch the ship, but Harry decided to stay with the Nawab. Since the Nawab appeared to be involved with gangs of robbers, the British officials did not approve of him, and they threatened to take control of Khatm. Douglas asked Olivia to go to the mountains to avoid the heat, but she wanted to stay near the Nawab, so she refused to go to the mountains.

I, Robot

A Checking your understanding

Runaround

1 Ten years ago.
2 For twenty minutes.
3 Because of the low gravity.
4 Because the First Law said that a robot must not allow a human being to come to harm, and Powell was in danger.

Reason

1 T   2 T   3 F   4 T   5 F

Catch that Rabbit

1 The robot didn't work.
2 Because they were controlled almost wholly by Dave.
3 Because the roof of the tunnel had fallen down behind them.
4 One of the subsidiary robots.
5 In emergency situations.

Liar!

1 Because he wants to find out how human minds work and to learn about human feelings.
2 For thirty years.
3 Because that would break the First Law.
4 Because he was in an impossible situation – anything he did would break the First Law.

Little Lost Robot

1 T   2 F   3 F   4 T   5 T

Evidence

1 Because nobody had ever seen him eat, drink or sleep.
2 They cared for each other and helped each other. Byerley helped John with his physical strength, and John was the clever one of the pair who solved the problems they faced.
3 Lanning wasn't interested in whether Byerley was a robot or not – he just wanted to protect US Robots. Dr Calvin was interested in seeing how Byerley managed to convince people that he was not a robot.
4 Because robots can never be cruel, stupid, or unjust.

B Working with language

Exercise 1

6 & 4   9 & 1   5 & 7   2 & 10   3 & 8

Exercise 2

1 as long as
2 In order to
3 Although
4 and
5 however

This Rough Magic

A Checking your understanding

Chapters 1–4

1 F   2 T   3 T   4 F   5 F   6 T

Chapters 5–8

1 Godfrey Manning.

2 Because he didn't say anything about Yanni's visit to the Castello on Sunday night.
3 To get the diamond ring that Phyllida had left there.
4 Because he would die if his skin became too dry.
5 Because she was worried that he still wanted to shoot it.
6 They tied a rope round the dolphin's tail, tied the other end to the boat, and used the power of the boat's engine to pull the dolphin into the sea.

Chapters 9–12
1 Yanni.
2 Maria.
3 Adoni and Max.
4 Godfrey Manning.
5 Max.
6 Adoni.

Chapters 13–16
1 She used the spare key that Miranda found for her.
2 In the water in the boathouse.
3 Because she realized that Godfrey had seen her shoe and knew she was there.
4 Because he wanted Lucy to know how clever and powerful he was, and she wouldn't be able to tell anyone because he was going to kill her.
5 A young man from the next village took her on his motorcycle.
6 To get the forged money that was hidden there.
7 Because Adoni had done something to the boat – perhaps he had turned on the gas in the kitchen so that the gas would explode.

B Working with language

Exercise 1
3 & 8 & 5   9 & 2   10 & 7   1 & 4 & 6

Exercise 2
Model answer
When Godfrey found Lucy on his boat, she pretended that she didn't know anything about his secrets, but he did not believe her. Then she realized that he was going to kill her, so she hit him and fought hard. When he pulled out his gun, she jumped over the side of the boat into the sea, which carried her towards the shores of Corfu. It was too far, however, and she began to drown. Suddenly the dolphin came and pushed her towards the shore, where a big wave rolled her up the beach, and she fell unconscious on the sand.

Wuthering Heights

A Checking your understanding

Chapters 1–6
1 Catherine Linton.
2 The Earnshaw family.

3 Ellen Dean and Zillah.
4 On the streets of Liverpool.
5 A fever.
6 Hindley Earnshaw.

Chapters 7–12
1 F   2 F   3 T   4 T   5 F   6 F

Chapters 13–18
1 Because it was the same day that her mother had died.
2 Because all the Linton fortune went to her cousin Linton, who was Isabella's son.
3 She pretended to go to bed but then rode to Wuthering Heights to see Linton.
4 He tricked her into coming to his house, and then refused to let her go home until she married Linton.
5 Hareton Earnshaw.

B Working with language

Exercise 1
1 . . . because she was in love with him.
2 . . . after his parents died.
3 . . . until she married Linton.
4 . . . if Heathcliff hadn't won the house from Hindley in a game of cards.

Exercise 2
1 & 9   2 & 12   3 & 8   4 & 11   5 & 10   6 & 7

STAGE SIX

Cry Freedom

A Checking your understanding

Chapters 1–2
1 F   2 F   3 T

Chapters 3–5
1 He thought South Africa needed organizations where black and white people could work together.
2 He would go to prison.
3 White people.
4 It could teach them how to live together.

Chapters 6–9
1 Because he wanted to treat the Captain the same way that the Captain had treated him.
2 It was for black people to build within themselves a sense of their own humanity, their proper place in the world.
3 He gave them to his wife, who hid them between two nappies fastened on to their son Samora.

Chapters 10–14

1 He was now feeling a deep anger because he had learnt what South Africa was to a black man.
2 *Open answer.*
3 Anger, sorrow, pride, and determination.
4 Woods wanted to leave so that his book on Biko could be published in England; Wendy, however, was unwilling to leave their home but changed her mind when her children were sent T-shirts that burned their skin.

Chapters 15–18

1 Bruce McCullough and Father Kani.
2 Because there had been a lot of rain and the river was too fast and too wide for him to walk across.
3 Because they wouldn't be safe from the South African police there.
4 He arranged United Nations passports for them and sent John Monyane with them on the plane to Botswana.

B Working with language

Exercise 1

1 The police changed the place and time of road-blocks because news of them travelled fast.
2 The policeman threw the keys to his colleague and then shone his torch on to the papers.
3 He saw that the man's hands were tied behind his back and one leg tied to the bars of the wall.
4 He knew what he must recommend but he also knew that the prisoner was important to the police.
5 It was obvious to the doctor that the police officer wanted police doctors to deal with Biko.

Exercise 2

Suddenly   Understandably   luckily
although   No sooner   since   While

Deadheads

A Checking your understanding

Chapters 1–5

1 About eleven.
2 His company made toilets and sinks.
3 Because it had been damaged and it was at the garage being repaired.
4 Ellie offered Daphne a lift when she saw her outside Diana's school in the rain.
5 Growing roses.
6 A rose called Blue Moon.

Chapters 6–11

1 He felt that there was something wrong, and wanted to know how Aldermann, who wasn't very good at his job, had got so far.
2 A stone from Little Leven church tower fell on him and killed him.
3 Jonty Marsh and Mick Feaver.

4 Because he had been stealing money for three or four years from one of his company's customers – a rich old lady whose money he was supposed to be managing.
5 Because the buyer had died.
6 He discovered that they had been having an affair.

Chapters 12–16

1 F   2 T   3 F   4 T   5 F   6 F

Chapters 17–21

Open answers.

B Working with language

Exercise 1

1 . . . he thought Patrick Aldermann was killing people.
2 . . . leaving him to die when he had his heart attack.
3 . . . he had decided never to see him again.
4 . . . she thought Ellie had been spying on her.
5 . . . she was her aunt's only living relative and there was no will.
6 . . . hitting him over the head with a heavy silver candle-stick.

Exercise 2

While Patrick Aldermann and his family were away from home, six policemen spent the night at Rosemont. They were hoping to catch a gang of burglars, but nothing happened that night. In the morning Pascoe found Dalziel in the house, looking through Patrick's papers. Pascoe asked him if they were leaving, but Dalziel told him to wait, as they would catch the burglars first. When the gardeners arrived in their van, Pascoe realized that they were the burglars, and the police caught them. Shaheed Singh was injured in the struggle, but he was not seriously hurt, in spite of being hit over the head with a heavy candle-stick.

Dublin People

A Checking your understanding

Flat in Ringsend

1 Jo had dreamt of working in the big General Post Office in the centre of Dublin, living somewhere nearby, and having a wonderful social life in the big city with new friends. The reality was that she worked in a small local post office and had to travel through miles and miles of streets where nobody knew anyone, take endless bus journeys, and was too exhausted for a social life.
2 Pauline was a punk. She had brightly coloured hair and clothes.
3 Maura's boyfriend Steve had given the TVs to them for almost nothing.

4 That she was in a flat by herself, not sharing a flat with two other girls.
5 They had bought her drinks in the pub where she had gone to see The Great Gaels.
6 Because Pauline and Nessa did not return home.
7 A window in the kitchen was broken by a big stone and broken glass flew everywhere.
8 Mary's burnt sausages.
9 The bits of paper on which Christy and Gerry had untidily written their names.

Flat in Ringsend
Open answers.

Murmurs in Montrose
1 Gerry Moore's mother, his brother Jack, his children Paul and Helen, Father Vincent, his friend Des Kelly and Emma, his wife.
2 Emma had taken the alcohol out of the cupboard in the living room and Gerry thought at first that she had poured it down the sink.
3 Paul was embarrassed because his father was emotional, and also annoyed because he couldn't go to his friend's house. Helen was upset and worried that her parents would be fighting and saying awful things to each other.
4 Because the number of small debts was growing and Gerry had not earned one penny since he had come out of the nursing home.
5 He wanted to cheer life up a bit with someone else's champagne.
6 She decided to leave him in a year or two when the children were older.

Murmurs in Montrose
Open answers.

B Working with language

Exercise 1
3 & 7   9 & 1 & 10   2 & 11 & 5
6 & 8   12 & 3

By Saturday night there was still no sign of Nessa and Pauline, and Jo really believed that they had been kidnapped. At midnight she was still wide awake so she went down to the party in the nurses' flat, but she didn't enjoy it at all. The guards were called because somebody had thrown a stone through the window, and after that the party came to an end. When Jo fainted on the stairs, the guards carried her upstairs to her flat. Then they sat and talked with her over a cup of tea and in the end persuaded her that she was being silly.

Exercise 2
1 . . . because she wanted him to call in on the family that night.
2 Although Father Vincent was anxious to help, he decided not to visit on the first night.
3 . . . but he didn't want to drink any of it.
4 . . . until Gerry came home from the nursing home.

The Enemy

A Checking your understanding

Chapters 1–7
1 She wanted him to meet her family.
2 Someone threw acid in her face.
3 He wanted him to marry Penny as soon as possible.
4 Because he hadn't expected to find any information about Ashton in the computer memory.
5 He wanted him to guard Penny and her father.
6 He found a laboratory in the cellar, a small secret strong-room behind Ashton's bedroom, and an enormous model railway.
7 Because someone had searched her room.
8 Because he didn't like working on weapons, and he didn't like Russian society or the direction Russia was following after the war.
9 Because he didn't want to talk about his work on atomic weapons or work for them as a scientist.

Chapters 8–12
1 F   2 F   3 T   4 T   5 F
6 T   7 T

Chapters 13–17
1 He used his daughter's books and notes for his studies, and the model railway as a computer for his research work.
2 Because he thought Cregar would use Ashton's programs to increase his own power.
3 It proved that Benson had been working as a spy for Cregar.
4 Because he thought that something had happened to Penny at the laboratory.
5 He would let Penny be taken to hospital if Malcolm signed a document which would make sure he could say nothing about the laboratory.
6 Because the accident with the gun had released dangerous bacteria, and he didn't want them to get outside the laboratory.
7 Because he wanted to stay an honest man.
8 Because he wanted people to know what is done by governments in the name of 'the people'. He wanted them to know about Penny's father and his discoveries in genetics, so that people like Cregar couldn't use the secrets for themselves.

B Working with language

Exercise 1
1 . . . until Gillian had acid thrown into her face.
2 . . . although he wasn't allowed to tell Ashton what he was doing.
3 Because Ashton thought his daughters were in danger, he disappeared.
4 . . . unless Penny gave him permission.
5 . . . when Ogilvie offered him a new important job.

Exercise 2
7 & 11 & 2   6 & 4   9 & 8 & 1
5 & 13 & 10   12 & 3

Jane Eyre

A Checking your understanding

Chapters 1–2
1 Eliza, John and Georgiana Reed.
2 Jane's uncle, Mr Reed.
3 Bessie.

Chapters 3–6
1 F   2 T   3 T   4 F

Chapters 7–18
1 Mrs Fairfax.
2 In a room on the top floor.
3 Céline.
4 Blanche Ingram.
5 John Reed.
6 Her uncle, John Eyre.
7 Mr Eyre's lawyer.
8 Bertha Mason.

Chapters 19–23
1 Because she didn't want anybody to know where she had come from.
2 To become a missionary.
3 He could not marry Rosamund Oliver, although he loved her deeply, because he knew she would not make a good wife for a missionary.
4 She shared it equally with her cousins.
5 Because she didn't want to lose her freedom.

Chapters 24–25
1 F   2 F   3 T   4 F

B Working with language

Exercise 1
Jane was unhappy at school because she found it difficult to accept the strict school rules. Although many of the pupils caught typhus fever, Jane remained healthy and was able to enjoy walking in the fields and valleys. However, Mr Brocklehurst thought she was an example of evil, and she had to stand on a chair in the schoolroom as a punishment, even though she had not done anything wrong.

Exercise 2
1 . . . if he had not hurt her first.
2 . . . in order to make Jane madly jealous.
3 Before Jane heard of her aunt's illness, she dreamed of a small child every night for a week.
4 . . . because Mr Mason could prove that Mr Rochester's wife was still alive.
5 Although Jane was small and plain, Mr Rochester loved her more than the beautiful Blanche.

Meteor

A Checking your understanding

Meteor
1 They were sent out because their old world was dying, so they had to find a new home where their race could survive and develop.
2 They were killed by the cat on the floor of the outhouse.
3 Because they didn't know what kind of weapon had killed it.
4 They found soft dust which protected the inside of the globe from heat. Then they found soft plastic, which made the compartments that Onns and his friends travelled in. Next to that there were compartments containing tubes, seeds, and powders, which the creatures planned to use to make their new life on Earth. Last there was a ten-centimetre space – the central hall where the creatures met.
5 Some were killed by the fierce grey creatures they met in the tunnels. The rest were killed with insect-killer by Graham, who thought they were stinging insects.

Dumb Martian
1 He paid a total of £2,310 – £1,000 to her parents, £1,000 to the Company for her food, £10 for a marriage licence, £100 for a passport, £100 to the Agent, and £100 for clothes and other things.
2 He was annoyed by everything she did, and especially by the way she accepted the problems of their life without showing any feelings.
3 When he taught her to play chess and cards, she soon became able to beat him.
4 He treated Lellie as an intelligent person, which made Duncan afraid that he would lose control of her, and that she would want to stay with Alan instead of him.
5 She locked him out of the dome after doing something to the electrical system on his spacesuit, so when the power ran out, he died of cold. He first tried to avoid his death by making signs to Lellie to open the airlock for him. Then he turned off the electricity to try and freeze her out. Next he tried cutting a hole in the dome. Finally he tried to send himself to Jupiter IV by container rocket.

Survival
1 F   2 T   3 T   4 F   5 F   6 T

Body and Soul
1 A quarter of a day.
2 Fourteen.
3 Machines do it.
4 Terry left poison, a revolver connected to a time switch, and a trap connected to some radio equipment. Hymorell left a small bomb and a trap which would start a fire.

5 He realized that she had grown tired of him and wanted Hymorell.

B Working with language

Exercise 1

1 . . . because much of it is covered with water.
2 . . . after he bent down to listen to the Globe.
3 Unless you had seen the monsters lift the Globe, you wouldn't have believed it could happen.
4 . . . until they heard Alice singing to her baby.
5 Although she let go of the baby, it just floated in the air.

Exercise 2

4 & 1   2 & 5 & 3   8 & 6   7 & 9   11
12 & 10

Night Without End

A Checking your understanding

Chapters 1–3

1 F   2 T   3 F   4 T   5 F

Chapters 4–6

1 Less than five days.
2 He found that the top left-hand corner of the radio cabinet was badly damaged and that it had a small dark stain and some threads of navy blue cloth on it.
3 Two.
4 Because she was engaged to marry him.
5 To find the two guns that the murderers must have had.

Chapters 7–9

1 Because he knew that Mahler would die unless he got some insulin soon.
2 The newspaper article that he had taken from Colonel Harrison's pocket.
3 Because he had had to stop and clean the engine and purify the petrol that had had sugar put in it.
4 Solly Levin. Someone hit his foot, he tripped and pushed Helene over the edge by accident.
5 The stolen tins of meat were found in Zagero's bag, and the keys to the bag were in Levin's clothes.

Chapters 10–12

Open answers.

B Working with language

Exercise 1

As soon as the scientists heard the plane, they rushed out, thinking it was in trouble. The plane crash-landed, but it did not catch fire, so the scientists were able to rescue the passengers and take them to the cabin. However, it was impossible to call for help from the outside world because the radio in the cabin had been smashed beyond repair. As there

wasn't enough food in the cabin for thirteen people, Mason decided to take the passengers to the coast, although he knew it would be a difficult and dangerous journey.

Exercise 2

3, 6, 9, 1, 4, 8, 5, 11, 10, 2, 7

Model answer
On the way through the pass, Helene slipped and fell into the crevasse. Luckily, however, she landed on a snow and ice bridge six metres down. Jackstraw jumped down after her, hurting his arm as he fell, so Mason lowered himself down into the crevasse to help them. He tied a rope round Helene, who was then pulled to safety. As soon as he heard the ice beginning to crack, he and Jackstraw jumped to the other side of the snow bridge, and then one side of the bridge collapsed. When Mason looked up and saw Corazzini with a gun in his hand, he thought Corazzini was going to kill them, but Corazzini smiled and threw down a rope.

Oliver Twist

A Checking your understanding

Chapters 1–5

1 Nothing.
2 Because nobody expected the boys to be brave enough to complain about their situation.
3 Oliver, as a workhouse orphan, had an even lower position in society than Noah, so Noah was able to revenge himself on Oliver for all the insults he himself had received.
4 Because his only friend there was Mr Sowerberry, and when Mr Sowerberry beat him, Oliver didn't want to stay any longer.
5 Because he thought Fagin would be pleased to have another boy to train as a thief.
6 He thought it was an amusing game, though it puzzled him.
7 They thought he might tell the police something which would get them into trouble.

Chapters 6–10

1 Mr Brownlow thought Oliver was a good, honest boy, but Mr Grimwig thought he was deceiving Mr Brownlow, and that he would run away with the books and the money and rejoin the thieves.
2 Nancy and Bill Sikes.
3 Because he thought it was time to include Oliver in a crime so that his sense of guilt would make him feel he had to stay with the robbers.
4 She told her that she had stolen something made of gold from Oliver's mother when she died.
5 He made the servants feel confused about whether Oliver was the boy they had seen in the robbery.
6 She sold him a gold locket and a wedding ring for twenty-five pounds.

Chapters 11–14

1 She had gone there to fetch some money for Bill Sikes.
2 She told her that Monks was Oliver's brother and that he had the money Oliver should have got from his father.
3 Because he wanted to find out who Nancy's new man was.
4 He got Noah to tell Bill what Nancy had done, knowing that Bill would kill her.
5 Because Mr Brownlow promised that Monks' crimes would remain secret and there would be no charges of fraud and robbery against him.
6 They discovered that Rose was Oliver's aunt.
7 He was hanged.
8 Rose married Harry Maylie and went to live in a small village. Oliver was adopted by Mr Brownlow and they went to live in the same village.

B Working with language

Exercise 1

It was a cold, foggy night, after midnight, when robbers broke into the house owned by Mrs Maylie. She and her niece, Rose, were sleeping upstairs at the time. Two men, together with a small, innocent-looking boy, broke into the house through a window at the back. The boy was sent in first while the men waited outside. However the servants came downstairs and surprised the boy before he could move. One of the servants shot the boy in his left arm, but the boy was pulled back through the window and escaped with the two men.

The boy was found exhausted on the doorstep the next morning. Rose made the servants bring the boy into the house, and when the police arrived, Dr Losberne convinced them that Oliver had not been involved in the robbery.

Exercise 2

7, 3, 5, 8, 1, 10, 4, 6, 9, 2

Model answer

The next Sunday Nancy managed to keep her appointment with Rose, because Bill Sikes had gone out that night. She met Rose and Mr Brownlow on the bridge and took them down some steps to the river bank, where she told them all she knew about Monks. However, Noah Claypole had been ordered by Fagin to spy on Nancy, so he followed her to the bridge and listened secretly to the conversation. He was amazed by what he heard and ran quickly home to tell Fagin, who was so furious that he planned a dreadful revenge on Nancy.

Pride and Prejudice

A Checking your understanding

Chapters 1–4

1 Mrs Bennet, to Mr Bennet, about visiting their new neighbour Mr Bingley when he moves into Netherfield Park. The ladies cannot visit him until Mr Bennet has met him.
2 Mr Bennet, to Mrs Bennet, about Jane, who had caught cold on her wet ride to Netherfield. Her mother had made her ride, rather than taking the carriage, in the hope that if it rained, Jane would have to stay the night at Netherfield – thus being longer in Mr Bingley's company.
3 Mr Darcy, to Caroline Bingley, about Elizabeth Bennet's eyes. Miss Bingley was hoping that Mr Darcy's admiration of Elizabeth's eyes would have been lessened by his disapproval of her 'adventure' in walking to Netherfield, but Mr Darcy thought that the exercise had made her eyes even more attractive.
4 Mr Collins, to Mrs Bennet, about her daughters. He is cautiously suggesting that a marriage with one of them might be possible.
5 Elizabeth Bennet, to Mr Wickham, about Mr Darcy.
6 Elizabeth Bennet, to Mr Darcy, about Mr Wickham. She is referring to the story that Wickham had told her about how badly he had been treated by Darcy.

Chapters 5–8

1 T   2 F   3 F   4 T   5 F
6 T   7 T

Chapters 9–12

1 Her character was similar to Lydia's, and they had been friends for two months.
2 She admired the owner's good taste and thought how she might have been mistress of Pemberley.
3 They were afraid that Wickham and Lydia might not get married but live together instead, thus ruining Lydia's reputation.
4 He played a large part in arranging the wedding, and went there in order to make a final payment to Wickham.
5 Because she wanted Darcy to marry her own daughter, and she also thought that Elizabeth was socially inferior.

B Working with language

Exercise 1

1 . . . as she assumed that Darcy would have told her all about it, because of the mutual affection between them.
2 . . . provided that he married Lydia as soon as possible.

3 . . . because he said scarcely anything to her and appeared more thoughtful and less anxious to please than in Derbyshire.
4 . . . so she took every opportunity to leave him alone with Jane.
5 . . . after he had proposed to Jane and been accepted.

Exercise 2
5 & 1 & 8 14 & 4 & 11 3 & 9 & 13
12 & 10 & 6 2 & 7

Model answer
Lady Catherine came straight to Longbourn to order Elizabeth not to marry Darcy, but Elizabeth refused to obey her. When Darcy visited Longbourn House a few days later, Elizabeth could not stop herself from thanking him for his great kindness to Lydia. Although Darcy had wanted to keep his involvement in Lydia's wedding secret, he took the opportunity to explain that his main motive in helping Lydia had been his desire to bring happiness to Elizabeth. Fortunately, he repeated his proposal, and Elizabeth was able to tell him that she now felt very differently about him. As a result they became engaged, to the delight of both their families.

Tess of the d'Urbervilles

A Checking your understanding

Chapters 1–5
1 Because he had an old silver spoon and an old seal.
2 Because her father made a fool of himself, and because the young stranger didn't choose her to dance with him.
3 Because the post carriage drove into Tess's waggon in the dark and hurt Prince badly.

Chapters 6–7
1 About four months.
2 Punishment awaits you.
3 Sorrow.
4 Talbothays.

Chapters 8–11
1 F   2 F   3 F   4 T

Chapters 12–16
1 He was thoughtful and honest.
2 She said she was not good enough for him.
3 Because she wasn't brave enough.
4 That she was a d'Urberville.
5 He did wrong with a woman in London years ago.
6 Because he felt she was not the same person he had loved.
7 Angel's parents would have accepted Tess and been kind to her.

Chapters 17–20
1 He began to change his ideas about what was right and what was wrong, and thought he had perhaps been unfair to Tess.
2 Because it had been in John Durbeyfield's name, so when he died they had to leave.
3 To warn him that Tess was in danger from Alec d'Urberville.
4 Because Alec helped her family, and persuaded Tess that Angel would never return.
5 In an empty house in the middle of some woods.
6 The police found Tess and arrested her.

B Working with language

Exercise 1
1 Although the other dairymaids also loved Angel, they knew that he loved Tess best.
2 . . . as he was sure she would accept him one day.
3 . . . in order to tell him about her past.
4 . . . since she had forgiven him.
5 . . . before he returned from Brazil.

Exercise 2
While Tess was working on a farm at Flintcomb-Ash, Alec d'Urberville came to see her many times and asked her to go away with him, but she rejected him again and again. Then Tess's mother became ill, and Tess went home to look after her. When Tess's father died, her family had to leave their cottage, and they had nowhere to live. So when Alec d'Urberville offered to help the family, Tess went back to him.

Answer Key
GREEN SERIES

Alice's Adventures in Wonderland

A Checking your understanding

Chapters 1–2

1 A watch.
2 Forty centimetres.
3 She got smaller, until she was only twenty-five centimetres high.
4 Some white gloves and a large fan.
5 A mouse.

Chapters 3–4

1 A caterpillar.
2 A bird.
3 The Queen.
4 The baby.
5 Alice.
6 The Cheshire Cat.

Chapters 5–6

1 F   2 F   3 T   4 T   5 F   6 T

Chapter 7

1 The Hatter was the first witness.
2 She was getting bigger and taller.
3 She wanted to cut off the Knave's head.
4 She woke up.

B Working with language

Exercise 1

1 Alice followed the White Rabbit when it ran down a large rabbit-hole.
2 Alice could not get through the door into the garden because she was too big.
3 Alice ran and ran through the wood, but she could not find the Rabbit's house anywhere.
4 The March Hare's house was large so Alice ate a piece of mushroom to get bigger.

Exercise 2

1 . . . it showed the days of the week, but not the time.
2 . . . she went through it, back into the long room with the little glass table.
3 . . . shouted, 'Off with its head! Call for the executioner!'
4 . . . she was much bigger than everybody in the room.

Anne of Green Gables

A Checking your understanding

Chapters 1–2

1 The station-master.
2 Anne.
3 Marilla.
4 Mrs Lynde.
5 Matthew.

Chapters 3–4

1 Diana.
2 Mr Phillips.
3 Gilbert Blythe.
4 Mrs Allan and Marilla.
5 Matthew.

Chapters 5–6

1 F   2 F   3 T   4 F   5 T

B Working with language

Exercise 1

1 . . . she thought that it was a very beautiful name and that her real name was not very interesting.
2 . . . she bought something to change it to black.
3 . . . was sad and lonely.
4 . . . it was having a difficult time and all his and Marilla's money was in it.

Exercise 2

1 & 8   2 & 6   3 & 10   4 & 7   5 & 9

Huckleberry Finn

A Checking your understanding

Chapter 1

1 The Widow Douglas's sister, Miss Watson.
2 Tom Sawyer.
3 Judge Thatcher.
4 Huckleberry's father.

Chapter 2

1 In a hut in the woods.
2 Under some trees.
3 Jackson's Island.
4 In a cave.
5 In a little wooden house in the river.

Chapter 3

1 T   2 F   3 F   4 T

Chapter 4

1 He said that he was the first son of the King of France.
2 Because they were always getting drunk and making plans to get money out of people.
3 The King sold Mr Phelps the news about Jim for forty dollars.
4 The Phelpses, because they are going to take Jim back to his owner.
5 They thought that Huck was Tom Sawyer.

Chapter 5

1 A week.
2 Spanish Island.
3 Because he had a bullet in his leg.
4 Because he wanted the adventure.
5 Because he was dead.
6 Because Aunt Sally wanted him to live with her.

B Working with language

Exercise 1

1 . . . he had to wear new clothes and be good all the time.
2 . . . Pop went into town.
3 . . . Jim ran away.
4 . . . he didn't want people to know who he was.
5 . . . jumped into the water.
6 . . . she thought he was Tom Sawyer.

Exercise 2

1 Widow Douglas was kind, but Huck ran away.
2 Huck found the canoe one morning when he went to catch some fish for breakfast.
3 There were no slaves in Ohio so Huck and Jim decided to go there.
4 The woman knew that Huck was there because the dogs made a noise.
5 Huck and Tom got Jim out of the hut and then they ran down to the river.

Robinson Crusoe

A Checking your understanding

Chapters 1–2

1 Robinson.
2 The Turkish captain, Robinson's master.
3 Xury.
4 The Portuguese captain.

Chapters 3–4

1 To Africa.
2 To the shore of an island.
3 The cave at the back of his tent.
4 From the ship.
5 Somewhere off the coast of South America.

Chapters 5–6

1 T   2 F   3 F   4 T   5 F   6 T

Chapters 7–8

1 Two.
2 Under some leaves.
3 Because he first saw him on a Friday.
4 He was looking for a turtle for meat and eggs.
5 Because it was an English ship.
6 On the nineteenth of December 1686.

Chapter 9

1 Three; two sons and a daughter.
2 His nephew.
3 Because he did not really like a quiet life.

B Working with language

Exercise 1

1 . . . to Brazil.
2 . . . he had a field of corn.
3 . . . he had a friend to talk to.
4 . . . it was death for all mutineers in England.
5 . . . were dead.

Exercise 2

1 Crusoe was a rich man but he could not buy anything.
2 Crusoe gave Friday some trousers and then he made him a coat and hat.
3 Friday began to jump up and down because he was excited.

A Stranger at Green Knowe

A Checking your understanding

Chapters 1–2

1 The little gorilla, Hanno.
2 Major Blair.
3 Ping.
4 The Head Keeper.
5 His friend Ida.
6 Mrs Oldknow.

Chapters 3–4

1 T   2 F   3 F   4 T   5 T   6 F

Chapters 5–6

1 He put them into a basket and took them into the wood for Hanno.
2 Two hundred kilos.
3 His little gorilla.
4 A piece of bamboo.
5 The Keeper.
6 Hanno came across a tree over the moat.
7 By the door, when they were having breakfast.

Chapter 7

1 Ping.
2 Hanno.
3 Major Blair.
4 The Keeper, Ping (and perhaps Mrs Oldknow).
5 Mrs Oldknow.

B Working with language

Exercise 1

1 . . . it rained nearly every day there.
2 . . . to ask Ping to stay at Green Knowe for the holidays.
3 . . . they were angry or afraid, or if people ran away from them.
4 . . . pulled up some vegetables and put them in a basket for him.
5 . . . couldn't.

Exercise 2

1 Hanno was unhappy because he lived in a cage.
2 Hanno lived in an African forest before he came to the Zoo.
3 Ping wanted to tell Mrs Oldknow about Hanno but he couldn't.
4 Hanno dropped down from the tree and he jumped between Ping and the cow.

Too Old to Rock and Roll

A Checking your understanding

Too Old to Rock and Roll

1 Greg, to Valerie.
2 Valerie, to Greg.
3 Greg, to Dad.
4 Dad, to Greg.
5 Greg's friend Toby, to Greg.
6 Dad's new girlfriend, to Greg.

Invitation to Tea

1 F   2 F   3 T   4 F   5 T

Party Wall

1 Jenny, Duncan, Anna, and Russell.
2 Duncan, because it was nearer the bathroom.
3 Because he wants to walk past the front door of the house.
4 Because Russell has a very strong, deep voice.
5 Because she doesn't want to be alone in the house with Russell.
6 He hears Russell crying himself to sleep.

B Working with language

Too Old to Rock and Roll

1 . . . the unhappy policeman came to the house to tell them about the accident.
2 . . . he was out.
3 . . . he wanted to give Valerie and Dad more time together.
4 . . . were twenty years younger.
5 . . . she's only a friend.'

Party Wall

1 Daniel wants to know about the students so he listens to what they say.
2 A girl speaks first and then a man replies.

3 Anna's young man comes to stay when the others are away.
4 Jenny uses a lot of hot water because she has a bath every night.
5 Russell loves Jenny, but Jenny doesn't love Russell.

STAGE THREE

On the Edge

A Checking your understanding

Chapter 1

1 Jinny's father, Joe Slattery.
2 Tug.
3 The Man (Doyle).
4 Jinny.

Chapter 2

1 The Woman (Ma).
2 Jinny.
3 Keith Hollins.
4 Tug.

Chapter 3

1 F   2 T   3 T   4 F

Chapter 4

1 He had the same ice-blue eyes as his mother, although his hair was black, and not fair as in the photo.
2 Because the Free People were against the idea of the family.
3 Because she thought Tug was a prisoner in her own home in London.

Chapter 5

1 It was harvest day on the farm.
2 He wanted to run all the way along Ashdale Great Edge to Castle Rock.
3 The royal family.
4 Rachel Hollins told him.

B Working with language

Exercise 1

1 & 6   2 & 5   3 & 8   4 & 7

Exercise 2

1 . . . wanted to stop Harriet warning the police about their plan to bomb the royal family.
2 . . . that his hair was now black, not fair.
3 . . . he had shouted for help through the window.
4 . . . drove north to talk to Jinny and ask for her help.
5 . . . she threw it high up in the air and it fell over the side of the ridge.

The Prisoner of Zenda

A Checking your understanding

Chapters 1–2
1 Rose, who is Robert's wife and Rudolf's sister-in-law.
2 Rudolf Rassendyll.
3 Rudolf, the King of Ruritania.

Chapters 3–4
1 Sapt.
2 Black Michael, the Duke of Strelsau.
3 Princess Flavia.
4 Sapt and Rudolf Rassendyll.

Chapters 5–6
1 To pretend to be King Rudolf, in order to stop Duke Michael becoming King.
2 He was losing his heart to Princess Flavia.
3 He knocked Duke Michael's men down with a tea-table and then escaped over the wall by a ladder.

Chapters 7–9
1 F   2 T   3 F   4 T

Chapters 10–11
1 He swam to it.
2 Five.
3 Johann.

Chapters 12–13
1 Because he was busy fighting at the Duke's side.
2 Because Rupert had killed Duke Michael of Strelsau.
3 To kill him.
4 She refused to stay at Tarlenheim House and rode at once to the castle of Zenda.

B Working with language

Exercise 1
1 . . . the King of Ruritania looked just like Rudolf Rassendyll, and Rudolf Rassendyll looked just like the King.
2 . . . she told Rudolf about Duke Michael's plan to kill him, and tried to tell him where the King's prison was.
3 . . . but Rudolf refused.

Exercise 2
1 Rudolf was a Rassendyll but he had the Elphberg hair and nose.
2 The King had disappeared when Sapt and Rudolf arrived back at the house in the forest.
3 Rudolf put his hands behind his back because he didn't want to shake hands with Rupert.
4 'They will kill the King and then they will push his body down the pipe.'

The Railway Children

A Checking your understanding

Chapters 1–2
1 Bobbie.
2 The children's mother.
3 Peter.
4 The Station Master.

Chapters 3–4
1 T   2 F   3 F   4 T

Chapters 5–6
1 Trees, grass, stones, and a big rock.
2 Phyllis and Bobbie.
3 A beautiful gold watch each.
4 Mrs Ransome.
5 A pound.
6 Perks.

Chapters 7–8
1 She read that her father was a spy and would be in prison for five years.
2 She asked him if he could find out the name of the real spy and so help get their father out of prison.
3 He broke his leg.
4 Because they saw that he was their own old gentleman.

Chapter 9
1 Hands and handkerchiefs and newspapers waved from every window.
2 Because she had a strange feeling that something was going to happen and she found it hard to think about her lessons.
3 A woman with three boxes of chickens, a woman with a brown suitcase, and the children's father.

B Working with language

Exercise 1
1 They couldn't buy the special food for Mother because they were too poor.
2 'It's true that we're poor but you must not tell everyone.'
3 People in the village liked Mr Perks so they were happy to give him birthday presents.
4 Bobbie screamed when the third person got off the 11.45 train.

Exercise 2
7, 3, 4, 1, 6, 2, 5

The Secret Garden

A Checking your understanding

Chapter 1

1 Mary's mother.
2 Mary.
3 Basil.
4 Mrs Medlock.

Chapter 2

1 Martha.
2 Dickon, Martha's brother.
3 Mr Craven.
4 Old Ben Weatherstaff.

Chapters 3–4

1 F   2 F   3 T   4 T

Chapters 5–6

1 She followed the sound of crying to Colin's room.
2 He was building a nest.
3 To see if it was straight.

Chapters 7–8

1 Because he went to the garden with Mary and Dickon nearly every day, and playing and working outside, and eating good Yorkshire food, made him strong.
2 His young wife.
3 Because of his dream, and because he received a letter from Susan Sowerby, asking him to come home.

B Working with language

Exercise 1

1 & 9   2 & 10   3 & 8   4 & 12   5 & 7   6 & 11

Exercise 2

1 . . . it was Mrs Craven's favourite garden and she had had an accident there which killed her. After that, Mr Craven hated the garden and wouldn't let anyone go into it.
2 . . . she found Mary wandering around the house and not in her room.
3 . . . he said she could take as much as she wanted.
4 . . . he walked all the way round the garden.
5 . . . was wandering round the most beautiful places in Europe.
6 . . . they walked back to the house side by side.

The Eagle of the Ninth

A Checking your understanding

Chapters 1–2

1 He had disappeared with the Ninth Legion.
2 He took fifty men out to meet the patrol, because the patrol would never get back into the fort without help.
3 To his Uncle Aquila's house, in the Roman city of Calleva.
4 He made the 'thumbs-up' sign.
5 A wolf cub.

Chapters 3–5

1 Cottia.
2 Uncle Aquila.
3 Claudius Hieronimanius, the Legate of the Sixth Legion.
4 Marcus.
5 Guern the hunter.
6 Some of his own men – soldiers of the Ninth Legion.

Chapters 6–7

1 T   2 F   3 F   4 T   5 F

Chapters 8–10

1 He brought food for them to eat, and he led them through the mist on a secret way across a bog.
2 Because, when Marcus and Esca climbed the tower, a big black bird had flown away, screaming loudly as it went.
3 Because, if he didn't say it, Marcus said he would throw the Eagle into the Lake and nobody would ever find it again.
4 His father's ring, because Marcus was brave like his father.
5 It was buried with honour under Uncle Aquila's house at Calleva.

B Working with language

Exercise 1

5 & 3   2 & 7   6 & 1 & 4

Exercise 2

1 Marcus bought Esca because he needed a slave.
2 Esca was taken as a slave when the Romans defeated his tribe.
3 Marcus gave Esca his freedom before they went to Caledonia.
4 He could not ask a slave to go with him, but he could ask a friend.
5 Marcus asked Cottia to keep his Legion's bracelet until he came back.

Gulliver's Travels

A Checking your understanding

Chapters 1–4

1 F   2 T   3 F   4 T   5 F

Chapters 5–9

1 He cut open the rat's stomach with his sword.
2 Glumdalclitch, the daughter of Gulliver's master.
3 Because he received a good price for him and was sure that Gulliver would not live longer than a month.
4 The Queen's dwarf, flies, a small white dog, and a monkey.
5 Because he didn't want to know how to murder people.

Chapters 10–12

1 Music and mathematics.
2 The professors wrote mathematical questions and answers on paper, then the students ate the paper.
3 They were all ghosts.
4 A human being who will never die but will live for ever.
5 They were called Yahoos and looked like human beings.
6 He didn't understand lying, war, or money.

B Working with language

Exercise 1

1 & 7   2 & 5   3 & 6   4 & 8

Exercise 2

1 Gulliver escaped to Blefuscu from Lilliput because he had enemies there. The Lilliputians were going to shoot arrows into his eyes, and give him less and less food so that he would become ill and die.
2 The dwarf was sent away from the palace after he dropped Gulliver into a bowl of milk.
3 Gulliver spoke to several ghosts while he was on Glubbdubdrib, the island of magicians.
4 Gulliver loved the Houys so he planned to spend the rest of his life among them.

The Silver Sword

A Checking your understanding

Chapters 1–3

1 Ruth was nearly thirteen, Edek was eleven, and Bronia was three.
2 A guard's uniform.
3 A bar of chocolate.
4 A silver sword, which was a paper knife, used for opening letters.
5 Jan.

Chapters 4–7

1 Edek.
2 Ruth.
3 Food, clothes, blankets, pencils and paper; she also asked him to find Edek.
4 Ivan the guard.
5 Enough food for a day, two blankets, Jimpy the cockerel, and the wooden box with the sword in it.
6 Jan.

Chapters 8–10

1 F   2 T   3 T   4 F   5 F   6 T

Chapters 11–14

1 Probably Jan and Edek, because Ruth and Bronia were nearly caught by soldiers and lost their paddle for a while.
2 Because Edek was now very ill and Jan had run away in the night, to go back for the silver sword.
3 He had caught Jan and Ludwig, who were in the back of his lorry, and he drove them all to the refugee camp near Lake Constance.
4 He had to choose whether to run after his dog Ludwig, whom he loved very much, or whether to go and help Ruth save Edek's life.
5 Her mother.
6 He gave it to Mrs Balicki, and said she could keep it for ever if she would be his mother.

B Working with language

Exercise 1

4, 6, 2, 7, 3, 5, 1

Exercise 2

1 . . . Edek hadn't done anything wrong / it was Jan who had changed the signal and stopped the train.
2 . . . made a sudden run for the door, and two guards had to bring him back, kicking and biting.
3 . . . sent the guards outside.
4 . . . Jan had to go to prison for seven days.
5 . . . invited them all into the farmhouse for a bit of breakfast.
6 . . . thought that Edek was not strong enough to work outside.

A Tale of Two Cities

A Checking your understanding

Chapters 1–4

1 Mr Jarvis Lorry.
2 Dr Manette, Lucie's father.
3 Charles Darnay.
4 Sydney Carton, a lawyer and Mr Stryver's assistant.
5 Gaspard.
6 The Marquis of Evrémonde.

Chapters 5–7

1 He asked her to remember that he would give his life to keep someone she loved alive and close to her.
2 His real name, which was the Marquis of Evrémonde.
3 He brought the news that Gaspard, whose child had been killed by the Marquis's coach, had been caught and hanged in the village near the Marquis's castle.
4 Because she was knitting a list of all the names of the enemies of the people.
5 Because his old servant, Monsieur Gabelle, was in prison and had written to him asking for help.

Chapters 8–10

1 F   2 F   3 T   4 F   5 T

Chapters 11–13

1 Because the Evrémonde brothers had caused the deaths of her sister, her sister's husband, her father, and her brother.
2 Because his mind had returned to the past again. He did not recognize his friends and wanted only to find his old table and to make shoes.
3 He made Darnay write down the message, and then, when Darnay was unconscious, Carton pushed the note inside Darnay's pocket. So it was carried out of the prison with Darnay.
4 Charles Darnay, but he was travelling under the name of Sydney Carton.
5 Because she was lying dead at the Manettes' home, killed by her own gun when she was fighting Miss Pross.
6 Because he loved Lucie and wanted to give his life to save someone that she loved. / Because he knew that he was doing a far better thing than he had ever done before.

B Working with language

Exercise 1

5 & 1   4 & 8   2 & 6   10 & 3   9 & 7

Exercise 2

1 ... he had been a prisoner in the Bastille, and everybody knew about him and how he had suffered.
2 ... lived every moment in great fear.
3 ... he was able to visit Darnay regularly.
4 ... these words had a happy effect on the crowd, and those who had shouted for his death now shouted for his life.
5 ... on the same evening he was again arrested and taken to prison.

Treasure Island

A Checking your understanding

Chapters 1–3

1 Because it was a wild, lonely place and not many people went there.
2 A seaman with one leg.
3 Black Dog.
4 He looked at the piece of paper in his hand, jumped up, and then fell down, dead.

Chapters 4–6

1 The blind man, Pew.
2 Squire Trelawney.
3 Black Dog.
4 Captain Smollett.
5 Long John Silver, the cook.

Chapters 7–9

1 F   2 T   3 F   4 T   5 F

Chapters 10–12

1 Hunter and Dr Livesey.
2 Ben Gunn.
3 Jim Hawkins.
4 Israel Hands.
5 Silver's parrot, Captain Flint.

Chapters 13–15

1 Because they no longer wanted him to be captain.
2 Because there was an echo, and a ghost's voice does not have an echo.
3 Because Ben Gunn had moved it.
4 Because it was now useless.
5 Five.

B Working with language

Exercise 1

1 ... the pirates arrived at the Admiral Benbow.
2 ... he heard Silver persuade Dick to become a pirate.
3 ... the pirates killed them.
4 ... his wounds were not dangerous.

Exercise 2

5, 2, 4, 8, 7, 1, 6, 3

PHOTOCOPIABLE WORKSHEETS

The ideas given in the next pages by Bookworms authors include pre-reading, while-reading and after-reading activities. Many of them are based on activities in Jean Greenwood's book *Class Readers*.

The activities in Section C of the exercises in each Reader can often be developed into after-reading classwork or homework, and the introduction to the story (on the first page of each Bookworm) can provide useful material for pre-reading activities.

The activities given are for these titles:

STAGE 1

The Elephant Man
by Tim Vicary
>**Pre-reading:** Take a letter
>**After-reading:** A board game

STAGE 2

Sherlock Holmes – Short Stories
retold by Clare West
>**Pre-reading:** Elementary, my dear friends
>**While-reading:** The plot thickens

STAGE 3

Tales of Mystery and Imagination
retold by Margaret Naudi
>**Pre-reading:** Every picture tells a story
>**While-reading:** Happy adjectives and friendly nouns
>**After-reading:** Read all about it!

STAGE 4

Three Men in a Boat
retold by Diane Mowat
>**After-reading:** A game of Snap!

STAGE 5

Great Expectations
retold by Clare West
>**Pre-reading:** Dear Marj
>**After-reading:** Fourteen characters and a hot air balloon

STAGE 6

Night Without End
retold by Margaret Naudi
>**Pre-reading:** I name this book
>**After-reading:** Character Bingo
>**After-reading:** Summary jigsaw
>**After-reading:** Trial by jury

The Elephant Man

Aim: Anticipation of plot and the role of characters within that plot.
Time: 10 – 15 minutes

Divide the students into groups of four, and distribute a copy of the letter below to each group.

Put the following questions on the board or OHP for the students to discuss. Encourage them to speculate and make as many suggestions as they like.

Let the groups suggest their own ideas. Then they could share their ideas with other groups. You should not tell them if their guesses are right or wrong.

1 Where is Joseph Merrick writing from? Why do you think he is there?

2 Why do you think the Queen sent Merrick a wonderful card and a beautiful picture? What did the Queen write in the card? What picture did she send him?

3 Why do you think this is his first Christmas? He is an adult, so what happened at all the other Christmases in his life?

4 Why doesn't he remember having Christmas with his mother?

5 Why do you think Joseph now knows many famous ladies and kind people like Dr Treves?

6 Why is Joseph so happy now? What does that tell us about his earlier life?

The London Hospital
23rd December 1888

My dear Queen,
    Thank you very, very, much for your wonderful card and the beautiful picture. It is the best thing in my room, the very best, the most beautiful thing I have. This is the first Christmas in my life, and my first Christmas present. Perhaps I had a Christmas with my mother once, but I do not remember it. I have my mother's picture too, and she is beautiful, like you. But now I know many famous ladies and kind people like Dr Treves, and I am a very happy man. I am happy too because I am going to see you in the New Year.
    Happy Christmas to you, my dear friend.

    With all my love,
    Joseph Merrick

The Elephant Man

Aim: Selection, ordering, summarizing and assessment
of events in visual format. Creative response to text.
Time: 15 minutes preparation, 40 minutes playing time

Materials needed (per group of students):

1 board (see pages 52-53)
1 set of **F** cards (facts, for the 'What/Where is this?' questions)
1 set of **Q** cards (quotations, for the 'Who said this?' questions)
1 dice
1 small token or object for each student to move around the board (ask students to bring their own tokens, e.g. different coloured buttons).

Divide the class into groups of between three and six students. Distribute a board and the two sets of cards to each group. Go through the rules and make sure everyone has understood them.

Students may move around the board quite swiftly, so you may find it useful to say that the winner in each group is the student who has made the greatest number of complete circuits in an allotted time, rather than the first student to reach the final square.

THE ELEPHANT MAN BOARD GAME

Rules

1 Each player takes turns to throw the dice and move their token a corresponding number of squares around the board from Start to Finish.
2 If the player lands on a blank square, they simply stay where they are until their next turn.
3 If a player lands on a square with an instruction, they should follow the instruction.
4 If a player lands on an F or Q square, they should take the top card of the F or Q pack, read the question on it out loud, and then try to answer it. If they get the answer right, they stay where they are. If not, they go back two squares. The card should then be put at the bottom of the pack.
5 The other players decide if the F or Q answers are correct. If there is a dispute, they can refer to the number at the bottom of the card, which tells them on which page of the book they can find the answer.
6 The players must throw the exact number on the dice in order to reach the end.

The cards

To make the F and Q cards, stick each of the following in the centre of a 4.5mm by 8mm piece of card, and stick or write the appropriate letter on the back.

Card fronts (continued on page 54):

One day in 1884, Dr Treves saw THIS in the window of a shop near the hospital.

FACT (1)

Dr Treves gave the man THIS and he opened a door at the back of the shop.

FACT (2)

The creature had THIS over its head, because of the cold.

FACT (3)

Merrick could not walk far without THIS.

FACT (5)

Dr Treves gave Merrick THIS with his name on.

FACT (12)

When Merrick came back to London from Belgium, at first the police put him HERE.

FACT (14)

Because of the £50,000, Merrick could live HERE for all his life.

FACT (16)

The new nurse screamed and dropped the food on THIS.

FACT (18)

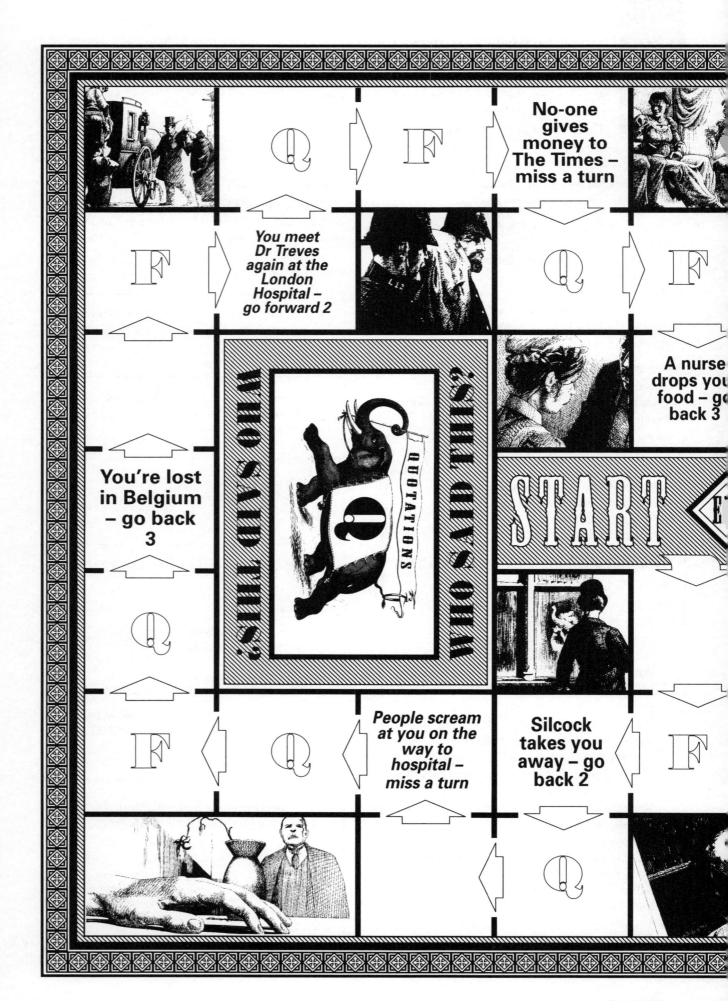

Q → F → **No-one gives money to The Times – miss a turn**

F → *You meet Dr Treves again at the London Hospital – go forward 2*

Q → F

A nurse drops your food – go back 3

WHO SAID THIS?

QUOTATIONS

WHO SAID THIS?

START

You're lost in Belgium – go back 3

Q

F ← Q ← *People scream at you on the way to hospital – miss a turn*

Silcock takes you away – go back 2 ← F

Q

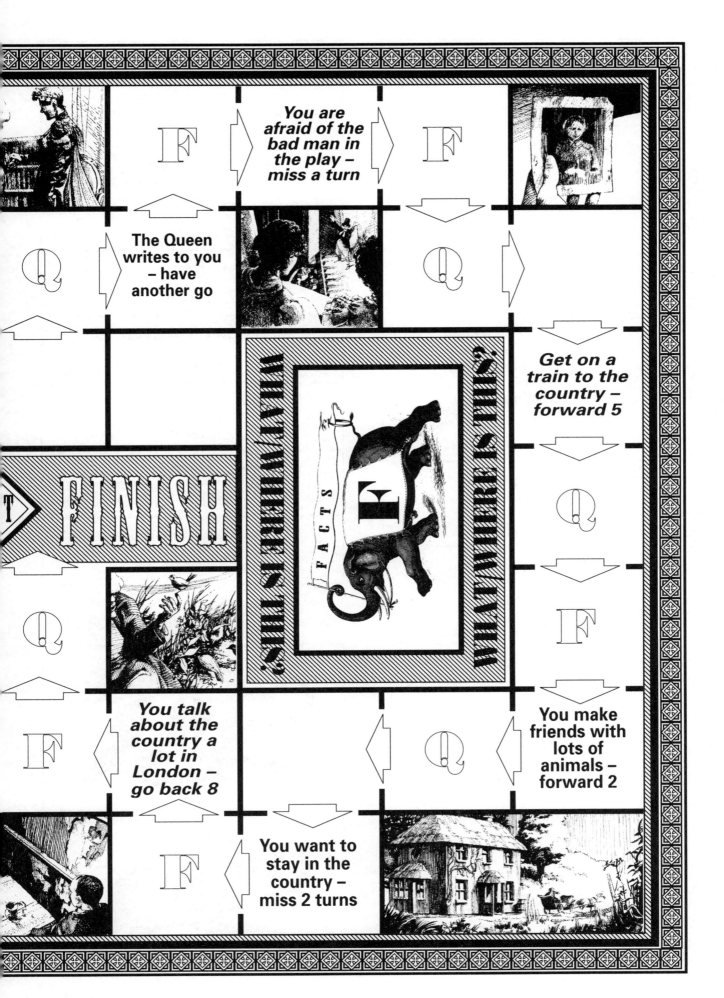

You are afraid of the bad man in the play – miss a turn

The Queen writes to you – have another go

Get on a train to the country – forward 5

FINISH

FACTS

You talk about the country a lot in London – go back 8

You make friends with lots of animals – forward 2

You want to stay in the country – miss 2 turns

THIS ran out of Merrick's eye and down the skin of his enormous, ugly face.

FACT (19)

Merrick would like to live HERE or HERE after the hospital.

FACT (19)

Merrick tried to get down on THESE when he met the Queen.

FACT (25)

Merrick had a lot of friends, but he was more like THIS than a man.

FACT (29)

In the morning, hundreds of THESE sang in the trees.

FACT (31)

The water in THIS made a beautiful noise, like singing.

FACT (33)

Here, this is my card.

QUOTATION (12)

I would like to live in a lighthouse.

QUOTATION (19)

A fat lady in a black coat!

QUOTATION (10)

It's very beautiful, isn't it?

QUOTATION (31)

What do you think they did after we left?

QUOTATION (30)

All right, sir. Give me twelve pence.

QUOTATION (2)

Do you want more money? Is that it?

QUOTATION (7)

Walk, Merrick!

QUOTATION (5)

Elpmyupasteps.

QUOTATION (9)

I'd like to see the Elephant Man, please.

QUOTATION (2)

No, please, Mr Merrick, do get up.

QUOTATION (25)

Hello, sir. Can I help you?

QUOTATION (10)

Nothing is easy for you, is it?

QUOTATION (12)

I think it looks like me, doesn't it?

QUOTATION (27)

Card backs: you will need 14 of each.

Sherlock Holmes Short Stories

Aim: To build interest in the stories by drawing on students' own knowledge of genre and character, to speculate about possible plots.

Time: 20 – 30 minutes

Draw a silhouette of Sherlock Holmes on the blackboard, or show the illustration below.

Draw attention, for example, to the deerstalker hat, the pipe, and the foggy atmosphere to elicit the name of the detective. Ask students to tell you how they knew who it was, feeding in new vocabulary.

Alternatively, invite the students to give you the names of famous detectives in films and books, eliciting that of Sherlock Holmes. Then ask students to tell you what associations they make with this well-known character. Focus on clothes, where he lives, companions, the types of investigations he normally undertakes (murder, blackmail, mystery, intrigue) and why (great intelligence, incompetence of police, attention to detail when looking at clues).

Then put students into groups of four to five, and give them the titles of the three short stories. They will probably need to use a dictionary to find out the meaning of some of the words.

> **The Speckled Band**
> **A Scandal in Bohemia**
> **The Five Orange Pips**

Ask students to guess what they think the stories might be about. Each group could write down their ideas, and then exchange them in a full class group. Do not tell students if their guesses are right or wrong.

Sherlock Holmes Short Stories

Aim: To check understanding of the story so far, and anticipate plot development.
Time: 30 minutes (for each of the three stories)

After reading up to a particular point in the story, divide students into groups and ask them to consider what could happen next to the main characters. They should decide which statements are correct, and choose the most likely outcome, giving reasons for their choice. It is advisable not to tell them whether their guesses are right or wrong, so that interest in continuing with the Reader is fully maintained.

The Speckled Band

After reading Chapter 1
(pp. 1–6)

Helen
Stoner ...

... will keep a wild animal in her room to kill anyone
who tries to hurt her

... will leave her stepfather and live alone

... will die soon, like her sister

... murdered her sister and will go to prison

... will marry and be happy

... will sleep in a hotel from now on

... something different

Helen's
stepfather ...

... is planning to murder Helen

... is going to hurt Sherlock Holmes

... keeps wild animals which will suddenly kill him

... whistles secretly to his friends the gipsies at night

... murdered Julia with the gipsies' help

... killed his wife (it wasn't an accident) so will go to prison

... something different

Sherlock Holmes ...

... will talk to the gipsies

... is planning to kill the wild animals

... is going to ask Helen's stepfather some questions

... already knows what the speckled band is

... will kill Helen's stepfather in the end

... wants to stop Helen dying like her sister

... something different

A Scandal in Bohemia

After reading Chapter 1
(pp. 14–18)

King Wilhelm von Ormstein ...
... will kill himself because of the scandal
... will marry Clotilde because she will never know about Irene
... will marry Irene because he loves her
... will kill Irene because she won't give back the photograph
... something different

Irene Adler ...
... will fall in love with Sherlock Holmes
... will give back the photograph to the King
... will ask for a lot of money for the photograph
... only wants to marry the King
... only wants to stop him marrying Clotilde
... is cleverer than the King
... is cleverer than Sherlock Holmes (is that possible?!)
... something different

Sherlock Holmes ...
... will tell Clotilde about Irene
... will fall in love with Irene
... will steal back the photograph
... will ask the King for more money
... will send Dr Watson to find the photograph
... something different

The Five Orange Pips

After reading Chapter 2
(pp. 28–34)

John Openshaw ...
... will go to America
... will die on his way home
... will soon get another letter from K.K.K.
... is going to meet K.K.K. at Waterloo Station
... has murdered his uncle and father for their money
... is going to run away from K.K.K.
... something different

K.K.K. ...
... are Brown, Robinson and Williams
... are three men who have names beginning with K
... is a group of people who are planning to kill their enemies
... is a strange word meaning death
... are friends of John's who are playing with him
... is something different

Sherlock Holmes ...
... will kill John's enemies
... will discover who/what K.K.K. really is
... will ask the police to help John
... will need Dr Watson's help
... will save John's life
... something different

Tales of Mystery and Imagination

Aim: Perception of connecting details and clues found in visual information usually accompanying text.
Time: 30 – 45 minutes

Preparation:

1 Photocopy the illustrations below and on the next page, which are taken from the book, and mount them on card.

2 Then write or stick the five story titles on separate pieces of card, as shown here.

The Fall of the House of Usher

The Fall of the House of Usher

The Black Cat

The Masque of the Red Death

William Wilson

The Tell-Tale Heart

In class:

3 Divide the class into groups, and make sure that each group has a full set of ten illustration cards and five story-title cards. Ask them to decide which two illustrations they think belong to which story title. (Some will be easier than others, but do not tell students if they have made the right choice.)

4 Write the following questions on the board and ask the students to discuss them and make suggestions. One student in each group can act as secretary and write down the suggestions.

   – What, if anything, seems to be happening in each picture?

   – What kinds of feelings are suggested by the pictures – fear, sadness, enjoyment, gloom, horror, excitement, pleasure, terror, happiness?

   – What caption can you suggest to go with each picture? If there is a character in the picture, it might be a speech bubble or a thought bubble for that person.

   – Suggest briefly what you think each story might be about.

5 When you are sure that each group is clear about its ideas, then the groups can exchange their theories and opinions.

Tales of Mystery and Imagination

Aim: To explore the various meanings of adjectives in a collocation matching game.
Time: 20 minutes

The Poe stories are very rich in atmospheric description and lend themselves to lexical development. After reading the first two stories, *The Fall of the House of Usher* and *The Black Cat*, students look at a list of selected nouns and adjectives from the two texts and compete in groups to decide which adjectives can go with which nouns. At the judging stage this game can generate quite a lot of imaginative argument and discussion about meaning and context.

1 Put the list below on the board or OHP, or provide photocopied sheets. Divide the class into groups and tell them they have ten minutes to write down as many possible adjective-and-noun combinations as they can.

2 Tell them they can pick unusual combinations, but they must be able to justify or explain them afterwards. For example, can you have 'horrible water' (yes, if it is drinking water and has a bad taste, or smells of fish), or 'a silent scream' (perhaps you can have one in a dream)?

3 When the ten minutes is over, each group in turn says how many combinations it has got and reads them out. The other groups judge if the combination is acceptable. If they don't like the combination, they can ask for explanations and then take a vote on whether to allow it.

4 The winning group is the one with the highest number of acceptable combinations.

ADJECTIVES	NOUNS
deep	gloom
happy	thought
dark	
large	house
strange	
sad	lake
mysterious	water
heavy	letter
pale	
thin	family
soft	
ghostly	fear
silent	cloud
fantastic	
terrible	face
wild	hair
calm	
friendly	light
honest	story
violent	
huge	cat
horrible	dream
peaceful	
loud	sleep
evil	scream

Tales of Mystery and Imagination

Aim: Interpretation of events and writing accounts in role.
Time: 60 – 90 minutes

For this activity, students can imagine that they work for a sensationalist newspaper. They will produce a front page which contains articles describing the events in each of the stories in the Reader. They can therefore employ all the journalistic tactics necessary, such as additions to the story, interpretation of events, speculation of motive/outcome, and witness interviews.

Preparation:
Prepare a skeletal front page by dividing the space to accommodate the five stories. Prepare titles for each of the stories and set them out on the front page. The headlines below may be used.

In class:
1 Ask the students to decide which story is being referred to by which headline, and which characters may be interviewed in connection with each event. Then ask them to suggest generally what they would expect to read in each news item, and which part of the story would receive most attention. Try to establish how journalists might feel about each event – would they be shocked, horrified, pleased, afraid?
2 Divide the students into five groups and allocate a story to each group. Remind them of the journalistic

tactics mentioned above, and the fact that journalists have a way of building big stories out of very little information.
3 A second copy of the front page should be made. From this copy each individual story shape should be cut out. In each group appoint a sub-editor who has responsibility for checking grammar and spelling.
4 Make sure that each group has prepared notes on the 'angle' of their story and which witnesses to interview. For example, in *The Tell-Tale Heart*, perhaps the old man who was murdered talked to a neighbour before he died and described how afraid he was of the strange young man in his house. The journalist could then interview the neighbour and one of the arresting policemen. In this way, you can encourage students to extend the facts imaginatively, in order to make 'their' story the most horrible or the most shocking. They cannot alter anything that happened in their story, but they can extend or enhance it.
5 Each sub-editor, when happy with the story, gives it to the Editor (teacher) who does any final checking. The stories are then glued into position on the second copy of the front page, which can then be displayed or circulated for the students to keep.

Strange deaths of brother and sister

Animal-lover arrested for murder

Is this the most evil man in Europe?

The Rich and the Cruel punished at last

MAN HEARS VOICE OF HELL

Three Men in a Boat

Aim: Revision of events and key facts of the narrative.
Time: 30 – 40 minutes

Make a pack of 52 cards by cutting out and sticking each of the following words and sentences on a piece of card. The pack consists of two sets of 26 cards. The first set has a character's name, an action, or an object. The second set has pieces of information from the story, each one of which corresponds exactly to a card from the first set. The cards have been printed in sequence and should be read vertically, column by column, so 'HE was certain he had all the symptoms of a bad heart' and 'J' form the first pair of cards. This is also the first pair to appear chronologically in the story.

All the cards are combined and shuffled in a pack, and one of the following games can be played. The games are best played in groups of four students, so each group will need a full pack of cards. Once they have got the idea, students often enjoy making their own sets of cards.

Snap

1 Give the players equal numbers of cards, face down so that they cannot see them.
2 Each player in turn lays one of their cards, face up, in a pile in the centre of the table. If two corresponding cards (that make a 'pair') are put down one after the other, the player who realizes it first either shouts 'snap!' or puts a hand on top of the pile of cards. (The second method is less noisy!) That player then picks up the whole pile of cards in the centre.
3 The game continues until one player has got all the cards and is thus the winner.

Pelmanism

1 Put all the cards face down in parallel rows.
2 Each player can turn over two cards (in any position) at a time. If the two cards are a matching pair, the player keeps both cards.
3 If the cards are not a matching pair, they are turned face down again and put back in exactly the same positions. The next player then has a go.
4 The winner is the player with the most pairs of cards at the end of the game.

Gin Rummy

1 Each player is given eight cards, face down, and the rest of the pack is placed face down in the centre of the table. The aim of the game is to put down matching pairs and to get rid of all your cards.
2 The players in turn take one card from the centre pile, and either swop it for one of the cards in their hand, or discard it. The discarded card is placed, face up, next to the first pile.
3 The next player may only pick up this discarded card if it matches a card in his or her hand, thereby making a pair, and must then discard another card from his or her hand. Alternatively, this player may take an unknown card from the face down pile. He or she must still discard a card because each player must not hold more than eight cards at any one time.
4 Whenever a player can make a matching pair, the two cards are put down face up on the table, in front of the player.
5 The winner is the player who puts down four pairs first and has no cards left.

HE was certain he had all the symptoms of a bad heart.	When old ladies and gentlemen look at **HIM**, tears come into their eyes.	Montmorency got into the food basket and killed **THREE OF THESE**.
The three friends agreed that they all needed **THIS**.	Seven people had to help **HIM** when he put a picture up on the wall.	When they were waiting for a taxi, a crowd came to watch because they had so much of **THIS**.
Harris said you do not enjoy living in **THESE** when it rains.	While they were packing, George stepped on **THIS** and Harris sat on it.	**HE** had got lost once in Hampton Court maze.

Harris loved visiting **THESE** but 'J' wouldn't let him.	When they were cooking supper at Shiplake, Montmorency brought them **THIS** to put in the pan.	Oranges
		Luggage
HE did not want to tow the boat because he'd had a bad day at the bank.		Harris
	Harris said that he had had a terrible battle with eighteen of **THESE**.	Churches
		George
On the first night it took them a long time to fix **THIS** over the boat.	'J' likes **THIS** very much; he can sit and look at it for hours.	The cover
When the branch of a tree broke on the first morning, 'J' **DID THIS**.		Fell in the river
	They discovered that the fish in the glass case was not real when it **DID THIS**.	George's shirt
Because 'J' was laughing so much, he dropped **THIS** in the river again.	In Oxford Montmorency had twenty-five of **THESE** in two days.	Eggs
		A tin-opener
Harris said he was very good at cooking **THESE**.	**THIS** came down without stopping and the three friends decided to go home.	The tin of fruit
		A cat
When they stopped for lunch near Monkey Island, they found that they had not got **ONE OF THESE**.	The three friends went back to London by **THIS**.	The river
		A dead rat
		Swans
They got very angry with **THIS** and finally threw it in the river.	'J'	Work
	A change and a rest	Broke into a thousand pieces
One morning Montmorency tried to argue with **ONE OF THESE**.	Tents	Fights
	Montmorency	
When they asked him for water, the lock-keeper said they could drink **SOME OF THIS**.	Uncle Podger	The rain
	The butter	Train

Great Expectations

Aim: To anticipate character and relationships, to focus on dilemmas faced by characters in the reader, so that students can identify more closely with them.

Time: 60 minutes

This pre-reading exercise takes the form of problem letters written to an 'agony aunt'. This is a person in a magazine or newspaper to whom people write when they have a problem, to ask for advice. Divide the class into four groups, and give each group one of the problem letters. Each group reads its letter, identifies the problem, and decides what advice to offer. A letter of reply can be written, if there is time, or this can be done for homework.

Then set up a 'case conference' at which each group presents a brief summary of the problem they have been discussing and the advice they intend to offer.

Now ask the class to imagine the relationships that may exist between the characters concerned.

KEY: Unhappy = Miss Havisham
      Worried = Joe Gargery
      Miserable = Pip
      Lonely = Estella

Dear Marj,

   Thirty years ago, I was engaged to a young man whom I loved, and I thought he loved me. But, to my horror, he deserted me on the very day of our wedding, and I realized he had never loved me at all. I was ill for a long time after he went away, and I suppose I was never really the same after the shock of this terrible disappointment. Even now, I don't like to meet people, or take an interest in anything. I inherited plenty of money, so I've never needed to work. These days I hardly ever go out. I spend most of my time in my room, thinking about the past. The worst thing is that, even after all this time, I still hate him so much! I'll never forget what he did to me. He destroyed my life, and I can never forgive him for that. I'm so desperately unhappy, and angry. What can I do with the rest of my life?

                    Unhappy

Dear Marj,

   I've lived in the same village all my life. Ten years ago I married a local girl, whose parents had just died. She had a little brother, who had no other relations at all, so I offered him a home as well, and we three all live together. My wife is a wonderful woman, and I don't want to say anything against her. She looks after the boy and me very well - the house is always clean and she's an excellent cook. But there's one thing that worries me. She always hits the boy when he does something she doesn't like. And because she's very strict in her ideas of right and wrong, that happens very often. I usually try to help him a bit if I can, but if she sees what I'm trying to do, she gets even angrier, and hits both of us. Well, *I* don't mind that, for myself, but the boy's still young, and not very strong. If I say anything to her about it, she gets cross. And she's cleverer than me - I've never been able to explain my feelings very well. What should I do?

                    Worried

Dear Marj,

   I expect you'll say I'm too young (I'm twelve years old), but
I'm terribly in love with a girl who is a couple of years older
than me. She is so beautiful! The trouble is, she hardly seems to
notice me, and when she does, she just laughs at me! You see, I
know she's rather proud of her appearance, and thinks it's
important to look good. Well, I want to look good too. I'm not
bad-looking - I just can't afford to pay for fashionable clothes.
I know she's being unkind to me, but I can't stop loving her! How
can I make her like me, perhaps love me one day? Please don't
advise me to forget her. I don't think I can ever do that.

                                                        Miserable

Dear Marj,

My parents died when I was a baby. I was adopted by
a rich lady who, because of her own sad personal
experience, brought me up to hate all men. From her
I learnt that men were dishonest, and not worth
thinking about. Now that I'm in my teens, I'm
beginning to question her opinions, but I find it
very difficult to talk to boys, perhaps because of
what she taught me. Several boys have recently
shown an interest in me, but I just cannot get
interested in them. They seem very young and silly
to me, and I can't help laughing at them.
Unfortunately I have no girl friends either, as
I've always lived alone with my adoptive mother, so
I have nobody to talk to about this. I'm beginning
to wonder if I'll ever be able to fall in love, or
have a normal relationship. Please help me!

                                Lonely

Great Expectations

Aim: To revise names of characters, and some association of characters and events.
Time: 20 minutes

This is a matching exercise to help students remember who's who. In pairs, ask students to match characters' names (on the left) with their corresponding descriptions (on the right) by drawing lines from the characters' names to their descriptions.

KEY: A8   B7   C11   D1   E14
      F9   G2   H10   I3   J4
      K13   L5   M6   N12

After using the previous activity to revise who is who, ask students to imagine that all of the characters are in the basket of a hot air balloon. Unfortunately, air is slowly escaping from a small hole in the balloon. The students will have to throw out at least two or three characters, maybe more, to make the basket lighter and keep the balloon in the air. Ask them to decide:

a) which characters should leave first, and
b) which character should be the last one left in the basket.

Questions students might like to consider:

Which character do you like best?
Which character is most important in the story?
How would the story change if you removed a particular character?

Students can work in groups to support a character, putting forward all the possible reasons why their choice should survive the others. At the end, the whole class can vote on it.

A	Mr Wopsle	1	The husband of Pip's sister
B	Abel Magwitch	2	A rich lady who takes an interest in Pip
C	Mr Jaggers	3	Mr Wopsle's young cousin
D	Joe Gargery	4	The man who marries Estella
E	Mr Wemmick	5	A hopeful young man, a friend of Pip's
F	Mr Pumblechook	6	The blacksmith's wicked apprentice
G	Miss Havisham	7	A convict who is grateful for Pip's help
H	Estella	8	The village church clerk
I	Biddy	9	Joe's uncle, who takes Pip to play at Miss Havisham's
J	Bentley Drummle	10	A girl adopted by Miss Havisham
K	Miss Skiffins	11	Miss Havisham's London lawyer
L	Herbert Pocket	12	The man who pretended to be in love with Miss Havisham
M	Orlick	13	A lady, first engaged, then married to Mr Wemmick
N	Compeyson	14	Mr Jaggers' clerk, who lives at Walworth

Night Without End

Aim: Anticipation of plot and theme; imaginative discussion.
Time: 20 minutes

The back-cover blurb can often be used to arouse the students' interest and to stimulate discussion about the kind of story they expect. Below is the blurb for this title.

1 Hand out copies of the blurb, but do not tell students the book title.
2 Ask the students, in groups, to make suggestions and guesses about the possible answers to the three questions in the blurb. Do not tell the students if their guesses are right or wrong. The right answers are *not* important. The students' responses to the blurb are what is being explored.
3 They could also suggest the possible development of the plot, perhaps based on their experience of this type of story. Will there be any more deaths or murders? Will there be a love-interest? Will the 'goodies' or the 'baddies' triumph in the end?

4 Finally, ask the students to choose which of the titles below they think would be most suitable for the story. They must justify their choices and rejections based on their expectations of the story, and the interest of the title itself. If they feel that none of them would be suitable, ask them to suggest their own.

If class sets of Readers are not available, this activity can be done for several titles from a class library. Students, after these discussions, could then select the title they want to read, and afterwards report back to the class on how the story matched the various hypotheses given earlier.

On the Polar ice-cap, 640 kilometres north of the Arctic Circle, the deadly, icy winds can freeze a man to death in minutes. But the survivors of the crashed airliner are lucky – they are rescued by three scientists from a nearby weather station.

But why did the airliner crash in the first place? Who smashed the radio to pieces? And why does the dead pilot have a bullet hole in his back? The rescue quickly turns into a nightmare: a race through the endless Arctic night, a race against time, cold, hunger – and a killer with a gun.

A Journey across the Polar Ice-cap
An Icy Wind
Murder in the Polar Night
The Last Flight
Night Without End
Death in the Snow
The Weathermen
Arctic Adventure
A Race with Death

Night Without End

Aim: Revision of associations between characters, traits, events, etc.
Time: 30 minutes

1 Ask students to make their own bingo cards with the names of four characters of their choice on them. For example:

Helen Fleming	Senator Brewster
Joss	Johnny Zagero

2 They should also prepare small pieces of paper on which they should write one piece of information about each of the characters on their card and his or her role in the story. They do not mention the character by name. The piece of information that they choose could be either very straightforward or a little harder. For example:

> *This man is a famous boxer and is travelling with his father.*

> *The stolen tins of meat are found in this person's luggage.*

3 Place the pieces of paper in a bag, draw out at random and read aloud. If a student hears a piece of information which refers to one of the characters on the card, she or he crosses off the name. The piece of information they hear may be the piece they wrote themselves, or that written by another student. When all four characters on the card have been mentioned, the student shouts 'Bingo!' and repeats the information she or he heard about the characters in order to win the game.

Bingo card template:

Night Without End

Aim: Ordering, remembering what has been read.
Time: 20 minutes

If the Reader has a fairly complicated plot, in which a confusing amount of action takes place, getting the order of events right can make quite a challenging game. This can also be done as a while-reading activity, picking a suitable point in the story, and using only the summary cards up to that point.

1 Prepare cards, each with one of the parts of the summary given below. Divide the class into groups. Each group must have a full set of cards, so several sets of cards may be needed.

2 The aim of the game is for each group to place the cards in the correct sequence of events, according to the story. All the groups start at the same time, and the first one to complete the task correctly is the winner.

3 After checking that each group has the correct order, the game can then be continued as 'chain story-telling'. Each student in the group takes a card and tells that part of the story to the rest of the group, adding any extra information or details that they can remember. The most successful group will be the one still telling the story when all the other groups have dried up. (Students should not look at the Reader while they are doing this.)

4 Once students have done an activity like this, they can produce their own summary jigsaws for other Readers.

5 The correct order for the summary is:

1 = J	13 = V
2 = H	14 = B
3 = E	15 = Y
4 = M	16 = G
5 = Q	17 = W
6 = U	18 = N
7 = I	19 = K
8 = T	20 = C
9 = A	21 = P
10 = O	22 = X
11 = D	23 = F
12 = S	24 = R
	25 = L

A
Somebody hits Mason on the head but the only thing taken is the unread newspaper article.

B
When Hillcrest describes the secret mechanism over the radio, Corazzini tries to pull out a gun.

C
Mason and the others catch up with Corazzini and Smallwood, but Corazzini shoots Solly Levin.

D
Corazzini's behaviour while Helene is being rescued from the crevasse seems to prove his innocence.

E
Mason discovers bullet holes in the dead bodies in the plane, and survives an attempt on his own life. Joss tells him about the explosives.

F
The tractor goes out of control and crashes. Smallwood and Margaret fall out, and down into a crevasse.

G
Mrs Dansby-Gregg, trying to protect Helene, gets shot in the back by Smallwood.

Continued overleaf

H

The radio transmitter in the cabin is smashed, and the next morning the injured radio operator is found dead.

I

After this discovery, Mason has no doubt that three of the ten passengers are innocent.

J

An aeroplane crashes in the Arctic Circle, but the survivors are rescued by three scientists and taken back to their cabin.

K

Mason and Jackstraw meet up with Hillcrest, and plan an ambush where Jackstraw will try to shoot Corazzini and Smallwood.

L

Jackstraw pulls Mason out, but they decide to leave Smallwood to die in the crevasse.

M

Mason discovers that his suspicions about Margaret Ross were quite wrong.

N

Brewster is discovered to be missing, and is found dead in the snow.

O

Hillcrest tells Mason that the stolen sugar has been put into his petrol.

P

Zagero, believing his father to be dead, attacks Corazzini and kills him in hand-to-hand fighting.

Q

When the plane goes up in flames, Mason abandons the search of the passengers' luggage. Joss notices the theft of the sugar.

R

Mason jumps down on top of Smallwood, allowing Jackstraw to pull Margaret up to safety.

S

The stolen tins of meat are discovered in Zagero's luggage.

T

Mason makes radio contact with Hillcrest and learns about the international search party looking for the plane.

U

At the first stop on the journey to the coast, Mason accuses Mahler of stealing the sugar, and learns that he is a diabetic.

V

Because of this, Mason decides that Zagero and Solly Levin are the killers and ties them up.

W

Corazzini and Smallwood drive off, taking Margaret Ross and Solly Levin with them. The others walk through the blizzard, carrying the three unconscious bodies.

X

Smallwood sees the Marines approaching, and, taking Margaret with him, drives off down the glacier.

Y

Zagero knocks Corazzini down, but Smallwood then produces a gun, and the two killers are at last identified.

Night Without End

Aim: Extension of an aspect of the plot into a moral debate; role-play involving interpretation of character and summarizing events.
Time: 60 – 90 minutes

Some students might regard Readers of this kind as just 'escapist thrillers', and transposition of a moral problem from the story into a different context can increase involvement with the characters' experiences.

1 If students are used to role play or drama work in class, they might like to organize this activity for themselves, perhaps over two lessons. They could decide on the format and procedures of the trial; whether to rearrange the classroom to resemble a courtroom; whether there would be a time limit for the speeches and the examination of witnesses; whether there would be mandatory or optional sentences if there was a 'guilty' verdict; and so on. Some students might also want to make role cards to remind themselves of questions to ask, and key events in the story.

2 The trial is of Peter Mason and Jackstraw. They have been charged with the manslaughter of Smallwood, who was killed in the crevasse at the end of the story.

3 The class will need to divide itself into five groups:

 – the judge and the jury
 (Both judge and jury members could be allowed to ask questions about any points during the trial that were not clear.)

 – the prosecution team

 – the defence team
 (Both of these could consist of two or three lawyers, who take it in turns to examine witnesses and present the cases for the defence and the prosecution.)

 – the witnesses
 (All the characters from the book who are still alive. Some might be more sympathetic to the accused than others. Hillcrest, for example, was horrified when Jackstraw was intending to shoot Corazzini and Smallwood with his rifle, and might strongly disapprove of taking the law into one's own hands. Zagero, however, though he is not on trial here, might well be wondering if he himself will soon be charged with the murder of Corazzini. So he is likely to be very anxious for a verdict of 'not guilty'.)

 – the accused
 (Mason and Jackstraw, as well as answering the lawyers' questions, might also choose to speak in their own defence.)

INDEX OF TITLES IN ANSWER KEY

* = available on cassette